Conflict
and
Conscience

MARK O. HATFIELD

Conflict
and
Conscience

WORD BOOKS, Publisher
Waco, Texas

MARK O. HATFIELD

Conflict
and
Conscience

WORD BOOKS, Publisher
Waco, Texas

Contents

FOREWORD by Richard C. Halverson   9

PREFACE   11

Part One: THE MISSION BEFORE US   17

Dear Senator

19

Shalom

35

Out of Seclusion

51

The (Holy?) Spirit of '76

61

To Heal the World

75

Part Two: A LIFE TO EXPLORE   91

Searching and Being Found

93

A Living Dialogue
101

Part Three: THE QUALITY OF OUR LEADERSHIP   105
The Atypical Man
107
Authority vs. Love?
117
The Challenge of Excellence
125
From Curiosity to Commitment
129
Lives That Teach
137

Part Four: LIVING IN BOTH WORLDS   145
Living in Both Worlds
147

Foreword

Many contemporary religious distinctions are foreign to the primitive New Testament church. One is the dichotomy between the secular and the sacred. Followers of "The Way" in the apostolic church were accountable to God in all that they did. Whether it was eating or drinking, or whatever else, all was to be done "to the glory of God."

Another familiar distinction not found in the New Testament is that between the clergy and the laity. The Holy Spirit was promised and given at Pentecost to all the disciples, and Peter declared quite explicitly in his Pentecost sermon that the promise was "to all that are afar off . . . as many as the Lord our God shall call." All disciples were to be witnesses and because of persecution in Jerusalem "they were all scattered (except the apostles) . . . and those who were scattered went about preaching the word." The apostolic church was a lay movement. In the words of Elton Trueblood, "In the New Testament church every disciple was engaged in full time service for Jesus Christ."

The maximum impact of the church on the world is not the influence of agencies or boards, of councils or committees, of the clergy, nor even the community itself, basic as that is. The maximum impact of the church on the world is the aggregate of individual disciples, filled with the Spirit of God, who live wherever they are and whatever they do, with a full sense of their accountability to God and who do all they do to the glory of God.

The strategy of dispersion whereby the Lord of the church himself scatters the children of the kingdom as good seed—as salt which has not lost its savor—is the key to the mission of the church. Jesus Christ has his people planted everywhere—in all the organizations and institutions and social structures—and between Sundays, when the church as a corporate body is invisible, they are doing the work of the kingdom as they are equipped and led by the Spirit of God.

Senator Mark Hatfield is one of the finest examples of this supreme strategy of Christ. This book will reveal his sense of divine appointment to government, his accountability, not only to the people he represents, but to God himself, his desire to do all he does to the glory of God, and his humble dependence upon the Holy Spirit and upon all his brothers and sisters in the family of God.

He knows, often from bitter experience, the inevitable tensions a man must suffer if he is to "render unto Caesar the things that are Caesar's and unto God the things that are God's." He does not equate the way he must go with the only "Christian" way in all situations, nevertheless, he works under a profound commitment to Jesus Christ, his family, his brothers and sisters in Christ, and the work to which he has been called. Meanwhile he honors the convictions of others and respects their rights to disagree without violating the unity of love in Christ. In conviction and conduct he defies all the clichés and stereotypes with which nonthinkers so comfortably label everyone. He is simply a servant of God and man who at the risk of political vulnerability has been willing to expose some of his deepest personal thoughts in public statements and allow them to be preserved in this volume.

RICHARD C. HALVERSON

Preface

Recently, I was speaking with a friend who is a professor at an Ivy League university. "Maybe you should take all the things you say to the evangelical conferences and give them to the national media instead," he said.

His words pointed to an important truth. We shrink from sharing our deepest convictions with those who may be unfamiliar with or hostile toward them. Perhaps this is because people today are more certain about their doubts than they are about their convictions.

A hunger of the spirit permeates society. We long for the taste of credible and courageous faith which can become the sustenance of life.

People are not particularly interested in our ideas; they are interested in our experiences. They are not searching for theories but for convictions. They want to penetrate our rhetoric in order to discover the reality of our lives.

An unabashed candor about our deepest convictions will be respected if we convey them in an authentic spirit of humility and explicate them by the tested quality of our lives.

The words on these pages are my attempt to say "This is where I stand." I do not deal directly with political convictions. They are the consequences rather than the cause of my life's basic orientation. During my years in politics I have given hundreds of speeches setting forth my political philosophy. These views have become somewhat known, I suppose, through the normal activities of the press.

I have also spoken before various religious groups during these same years. Those occasions, naturally, may seem far less notable in the public eye. Yet those are the times when I have revealed with greater abandon the core of my life's allegiance, and from which, I hope, my political activities and philosophy have been motivated. These are the words and experiences that I want to present to you.

How do we relate the resources of basic allegiance to the situations and circumstances of individual and corporate life styles? Is Jesus Christ relevant to contemporary society? I believe the wisdom and compassion demanded to solve any of today's personal or societal problems cannot be found in any person or place other than in the power of God, working through a man. Such committed men can make the dramatic difference.

Viewpoints and statements found within these pages will elicit controversy and disagreement, I feel sure. It would be most presumptuous for me to assert that my position on these subjects is *the* Christian position and, thus, through such an assertion imply that any contrary viewpoint is unchristian. I can only claim that I have prayerfully considered each issue and am persuaded that my stand is the one demanded by my convictions. At times I have used biblical references to support my views but with full acknowledgment that each one is subject to interpretation and personal experience. As Abraham Lincoln was quoted: "My concern is not whether God is on our side; my great concern is to be on God's side, for God is always right." Furthermore, disagreement within and without the Christian community of believers should be possible without rancor or hostility. To experience enmity because of diversity of viewpoint is contradictory both to our Christian teaching of love for the brethren and to our political ideal of personal freedom in a pluralistic society.

So, let me share what is very personal, but what must be shared, both verbally and in relationships, if one is to grow as a person and be enriched in his faith. Such communication must be natural and not contrived because it should reveal the true self without ego, façade, or defense.

To write the totality of one's experiences or views concerning God and faith is not easy because both are always in the process of growing and maturing. Yet, I can declare certain decisive points of faith. I believe in the truth that Jesus Christ is the Alpha and Omega of life. Therefore, man is mortal and subject to change, whereas God is immortal. He is the same yesterday, today, and forever.

Please understand that I am not sharing a systematic theology but a simple faith in a personal, transcendental experience with Jesus Christ. My faith is both an inward journey to find the true purpose of my own life and an outward journey to be of service to others.

Love is the constant reminder that faith is a relationship between man and God and between man and fellow-man. God demonstrated his inestimable love to each of us through the life, death, and resurrection of his Son. We, as recipients of that love, can become transmitters of that same transcendent love to our fellow-man. This is the gentle mystery and the dynamic reality of love—true love that reaches down from God and outward to man.

I ask only that you accept these words as one man's attempt to communicate his own journey of faith to any who may sense the quest of the Spirit in their own lives.

In 1969 I was asked to offer the closing prayer at the annual Presidential Prayer Breakfast, an event attended by people from various walks of life from throughout our country and the world. I was uncertain about just what would be appropriate for the moment until the breakfast began, then I jotted down these notes as the basis for the prayer I offered.

Holy, Holy, Lord God Almighty—hear now our prayer.

We are grateful for your having brought us together, but let this time not be merely an annual occasion in our lives.

Grant us a realization of the possible impact of answers to our prayers—the impact on other people and nations.

Excite our imagination with all our potential to serve and love you by sharing ourselves and our resources with our fellow-man.

Burn into our minds a sense of urgency to mobilize our technology to conquer the enemies of man—disease, hunger, poverty.

Grant our president and all leaders of men profound wisdom to achieve peace in all parts of the world.

Purge our hearts of all sin, especially bigotry, hatred, and jealousy.

Teach us to worship not self, money, pleasure, prestige, but to displace ego with the love of Jesus Christ our Savior and you as our Father, God.

Send now your Holy Spirit with each one of us to guide and protect.

AMEN.

Part One:

THE MISSION
BEFORE US

Dear Senator

David Hubbard, the president of Fuller Theological Seminary, had asked me to speak at their commencement in June of 1970. I accepted the invitation several months in advance, regarding it as a distinctive and challenging opportunity. As spring of 1970 unfolded, the Cambodian invasion, the Kent State tragedy, and a massive resurgence of dissent were hurled into national focus. Further, I had involved myself in legislative activity in Congress aimed at terminating our military involvement in Indochina. Such an unforeseen panoply of events reinforced my feelings that what I would say at Fuller was particularly crucial and had to be developed with exacting care. I knew that throughout the evangelical community feelings about the Indochinese War were sharply divided. Criticism of my position, which I personally found to be very troubling, was coming from those within the church who found it difficult to accept me as a brother in Christ because I was against the war. As I prepared for the Fuller commencement, I decided to speak on all of these issues and focus on the reconciling love that should characterize the life of every follower of Christ. When I entered the auditorium to deliver the address, I was still filled with some trepidation. As I got up to speak, students in the balcony unfurled a banner reading, "We're with you, Mark." It was a gesture that I needed very much at that moment. The warmth and acceptance with which my words were later received and the sense of support conveyed to me by the Fuller community made it a time of deep and meaningful personal renewal.

Dear Senator

YEARS AGO ONE OF MY FA-vorite radio programs was "The Old Fashioned Revival Hour" with Charles Fuller and his wife. I particularly remember hearing Mrs. Fuller read letters sent in from listeners.

I, too, have received some of the most remarkable, disturbing, and memorable mail. So perhaps it will be appropriate to begin by sharing some of my recent letters with you.

Dear Senator Hatfield—fellow Christian,

I thought you were the man for the job of senator because we need Christian men in vital places. But, when anyone chooses to go against the president of our United States the way you have, that's where my support ends.

Yours in Christ,

Dear Sir,

A member of your Oregon staff talked to me recently and pointed out your strong religious feeling. I doubt this very much because you are against the military which guarantees religious freedom and democracy to this nation.

Yours truly,

Dear Senator Hatfield,

I want to make it clear that when I did vote for you, I did not cast that vote with the idea of making you more powerful than the president of the United States. You only speak for Oregon, sir. Why do you think you have the right to interfere with our president? Have you forgotten that God's way is to respect and honor those in authority? What higher power is there than President Nixon? God put him there. "Whosoever therefore resisteth the power, resisteth the ordinance of God."

Very sincerely,

Dear Mr. Hatfield,

Your encouragement of antiwar demonstrations and the riots that have come from such demonstrations are in fact treason for they give comfort and aid to our enemies.

I am in favor of shooting rioters that throw rocks from buildings and try to force their wills upon others by violence.

I and a lot of other Christian people are extremely disappointed in your performance in the Senate, for you who claim to be a Christian and have access to our Almighty God should have a better understanding of human nature and the evil in the human heart.

Sincerely,

Now, I realize this thinking is not typical of either the theological or political perspectives likely to be shared by this audience—at least I hope not. Yet I believe it is typical of a segment of those who claim the evangelical tradition —a tradition which I also share.

There is a theological "silent majority" in our land who wrap their Bibles in the American flag, who believe that conservative politics is the necessary by-product of orthodox Christianity, who equate patriotism with the belief in national self-righteousness, and who regard political dissent as a mark of infidelity to the faith.

Letters from these people are the most difficult for me to answer. For they call into question the legitimacy of my Christian beliefs on the basis of my political positions.

I am tempted, of course, to do the same—to doubt the authenticity of their faith because of their disagreement with my stance on the war. But I know that these are people who sincerely name the name of Christ and whose faith I have no right to judge.

But it is not only an element of the theological right that baptizes a particular political doctrine and equates it with Holy Writ. The theological left has done so as well.

The tendency is to take the latest political theme of the left, baptize it with whatever theology or biblical references seem to coincide, and then proclaim these causes as the unquestioned work of the Spirit.

In the most extreme form of theological leftism, the traditional doctrines of the crucifixion and resurrection are given an exclusively political application. What this means for us, we are told, is simply that old political systems must die before new ones can be born. A messianic political program is developed which is nurtured by the apocalyptic rhetoric of the New Left and which defines resolute resistance to the government as the mark of true discipleship. The political and social avant-garde automatically becomes God's covert work in the world.

In the first case, those whom we might call "Biblical Nationalists" begin with what is the revealed Word but never truly relate it to the political and social realities of our age. On the other hand, those whom we might call "Political Messiahs" begin with a realistic sense of urgency about the crisis in our world but too often fail to hear the authentic words of God over the din of their own words. And both the Biblical Nationalist and the Political Messiah set forth rigid political criteria as the basis for judging another's Christian faith.

I cite these examples not to maintain that our social and political attitudes should remain severed from biblical perspectives. On the contrary, I believe the evangelical community has as its most urgent task the developing of a responsible social and political ethic that takes with equal seriousness both the truth of Christ's life and God's revelation of himself to man and the crises confronting the social and political institutions of our age.

Carl F. H. Henry noted this fact in his volume entitled *The Uneasy Conscience of Modern Fundamentalism.* Dr. Henry pointed out that the gospel was for the *whole* man —questions pertaining to the reconciliation between God and man could not be separated from questions pertaining to the reconciliation between man and his fellow-man.

Dr. Henry maintained that the religious liberals had upset this balance by emphasizing human relations to such an extent that they lost sight of the theological basis upon which reconciliation occurs. At the same time, however, Dr. Henry argued that conservatives had upset this balance in the opposite direction. They were so obsessed with maintaining the spiritual and religious dogmas of the orthodox credo that they lost sight of its ethical implications and imperatives. Along with others, Henry urged the conservative theological community to rethink its obligations to the social sphere.

Many in conservative theological scholarship have now gone beyond the essentially negative and defensive psyche that characterized much of the fundamentalist movement of a bygone era. A positive defense for the revelationist and supernaturalist basis of the Christian faith has been rearticulated. Now there is unfinished business—most notable of which is the obligation to demonstrate that reconciliation between God and man has application for reconciliation between man and his fellow-man.

Evangelicals have lost sight of the fact that the great issues being debated today are no longer those pertaining to organic evolution. Now they are those pertaining to social revolution.

We can no longer afford the supposed luxury of social withdrawal, but must find viable means to relate the Good News to the turmoil of our era. And as we have addressed ourselves to the theological problems of organic evolution in the past, let us turn to the theological problems of social revolution in the present. To do less is to concern ourselves with only half of the gospel.

Just because many theological liberals have upset the balance between dogma and ethics in one direction is no reason for us to upset it in the other. Insofar as we preach only half of the gospel, we are no less heretical than those who preach only the other half. It is my hope that evangelical Christianity will be led in a return to the entirety of the gospel.

Outmoded perspectives have blinded us to the entirety of the gospel and shielded us from the hurt of the world. If we are to speak with a whole gospel to a broken world, we must first overcome this legacy which is illustrated in the following three examples.

First, we must call into question the unacknowledged alignment of conservative protestantism with conservative social and political interests. I grant, of course, that the evangelical emphasis on man as sinner puts limitations upon what we can hope for in the transformation of society. But let us not forget that Christ came to transform mankind and promised not only a new heaven but a new earth as well.

Christ gives us the taste of new wine and calls upon us to be his partners in reconciling the entire creation into a unity under God. While the fact of the fall places limitations on all human existence, the fact of redemption and resurrection provides new vistas and possibilities for all human existence. To teach either one without the other is to deal with less than the full message of the Christian tradition.

Second, we must reevaluate the faith we as a people have placed in the office of the presidency. Our democracy has evolved in a way that has centered increasing power and influence in the hands of the chief executive. At the same time we have also intensified the trust, confidence, and faith that we place in the man who holds that office. As evangelical Christians, we should be particularly sensitive to the dangers presented by such an all-encompassing trust.

It is not unusual for us to assume that the president is all-powerful, all-knowing, and the chief provider for our welfare. We Americans hesitate to question his judgment in military and diplomatic affairs; we are encouraged by his condemnation of those who displease us; we blame him if our pocketbooks are empty and praise him if they are full. We find comfort in his pledges to protect us from our enemies both within and without our land and believe he has a certain sanctity which is somehow defiled by those suspect citizens who question his leadership.

It is not about any particular president, but about the nature and power of the office of the presidency in our day that I am speaking. We should be sensitive to the potential of idolatry that exists when such a large part of one's security and trust is placed upon the shoulders of one man.

And we should remind ourselves that our theological understanding of the nature of man means that excessive power resting with one person will likely be used for self-serving and self-justifying purposes. Power shared by many —the premise of a democratic system—will more often be exercised with justice and wisdom.

Third, we as evangelicals must regain sensitivity to the corporateness of human life—we must become sensitive to issues of social morality as well as to issues of private morality. We must learn to repent of and respond to collective guilt as well as individual guilt. This becomes increasingly important as the structures of life become more interdependent and interrelated. An ethic which deals solely with personal mores is singularly inadequate if it fails to deal with war, poverty, and racial antagonism as well.

Jacques Ellul, the French theologian and social scientist, has remarked, "A major fact of our civilization is that more and more sin becomes collective, and the individual is forced to participate in collective sin." [1]

Can we not see that as life becomes more and more interdependent, the opportunities to participate in the collective good expand as well? We have recognized the fact that we participate in collective sin as individuals. Can we not also learn to participate in collective righteousness as individuals?

If we begin to rethink some of our traditional postures in areas of social ethics, we can then begin to respond creatively to the social and political crises facing our nation and our world—a world divided over wars in Southeast Asia and the Middle East—a world divided over drastically differing standards of living and economic attainment—a world divided by race and tribe—a world divided by ideology—and a world divided by the gaps between young and old.

Surely the gospel of reconciliation has something to say

to the divisions which characterize life in the modern world. Surely the Christ who befriended the Samaritan woman at the well, who cared for the sick, who fed the hungry, and who blessed the children—surely this Christ has something to say to us today.

As we consider the impact of Christ's gospel in these times, we must honestly confront the critical realities that characterize the life of the society and the world. There are three issues, distinct yet interdependent, which demand our attention: war, race, and distribution of wealth.

First and most obvious to us here in the United States is the war in Indochina.

As you may know, I sponsored legislation which provided a timetable for withdrawal of our troops which would extricate us from Indochina as quickly as possible. I am not asking that everyone agree with me on all the particulars pertaining to the question, nor am I claiming any divine sanction for my views. But I do ask that evangelicals join me in asking some fundamental questions as to whether our involvement—*our* involvement, yours and mine—in an effort being made in our name as an American people, and an involvement for which *we* bear the moral and legal responsibility—is justifiable.

I ask you to balance carefully and in good conscience evaluate the pros and cons to this endeavor and then have the courage to follow where your convictions lead you. Can we rationalize the human suffering, the wasted resources, and the deterioration of moral sensitivity associated with this war supporting what seems to be an authoritarian puppet regime in Southeast Asia? Is the good to be achieved in this endeavor greater than the evil we are being forced to endure to achieve it?

A criterion of the traditional "just war" doctrine is that the means be consistent with the ends being pursued. Again, those of you who are familiar with the My Lai massacre will be forced to ask some difficult questions. Here we have reports of Americans bayoneting infant children at the breasts of their dead mothers. Here we have vivid descriptions of American troops operating in "free fire zones," destroying all animal life at sight—cattle, sheep, and human beings alike.

What relation do kill-ratios have to our lip service about the value and integrity of human life? And how does our modern faith in superior fire-power relate to our national motto, "In God We Trust"?

I believe that it is morally indefensible to justify our involvement in Southeast Asia on the basis of national pride or to avoid national humiliation. The more we do so, the less we have to be proud about. A nation that can turn from its past ways, admit its error and truly seek a new path—that nation can discover a true greatness of spirit. Furthermore, grave constitutional issues are raised by the continued conduct of the war. It is imperative, in my view, that Congress restore the balance of powers set forth in our constitution by exercising its responsibilities for formulation of the policies of war and peace, rather than by abdicating those powers to the executive.

The spirit of both the questions I have asked and the answers have been molded by my Christian convictions. I can understand that others who share the same convictions may come to different conclusions. But I cannot understand how a Christian community can abide these evils without at least asking the questions which need to be asked, and without at least coming to some rudimentary and tentative responses to these questions. Let each of us discover how we must obey the command of Christ when he instructs us to be his peacemakers.

The second central issue we face as Christians in this age is the division among the races. Why has the church failed so miserably in dealing with this problem? Why is it that one of the bastions of racial hate in this country is located firmly in the so-called "Bible Belt"? Why is it that the overwhelming majority of evangelical churches are still segregated both in spirit and in fact?

There is hardly a better way in our country to demonstrate the love of God than by serving as an instrument of God's reconciliation among the races.

For all the talk about the ability of the voluntary sector to achieve what government alone cannot do, has there been any demonstration of this within our own community? Have we, individually and in our churches, acted in concrete ways to enable the reconciliation of the races? Too often we have not gone beyond the typical business corporation which employs "demonstration Negroes" as a façade to cover its racist underpinnings. I am convinced that God judges hypocrisy just as harshly—if not more so —than the overt racism which we all condemn.

Finally, there is the crucial issue of inequitable distribution of wealth, both in this country and throughout the world. An end to the war in Southeast Asia would free resources to help alleviate this problem. But I fear that if and when the war comes to an end, the masses will prefer a 5 percent cut in taxes.

Let us prepare now for that contingency. Let us commit ourselves to the goal of seeing that each person in this nation is granted the minimal resource for well-being which is justly his by virtue of his humanity.

Let us not hide from our duty by utilizing metaphoric excuses decrying socialism—creeping or otherwise—protesting the welfare state or painting pictures of big government as a type of antichrist. The evangelical conscience takes its authority not from John Locke's concept of property or William Buckley's concepts of strictly limited government, but from the New Testament. And when the two come into conflict, we ought to have the courage to follow in fact what we say we revere in our Christian dogma.

Even more difficult is the gap in economic and social well-being which separates this nation and those of the developed countries from the Third World. If we cannot muster the idealism to help these countries and their peoples as fellow human beings for the simple reason that this is morally right, let us at least stop demeaning them through paternalism for the simple reason that it is morally wrong. Let us share our resources with these countries either out of altruism or out of a realism which recognizes that the growing division between rich and poor in this world only escalates the frequency and intensity of violence.

Each of these issues—the war, racial antagonism, and the disparity between rich and poor—contains the seeds of our own destruction and jeopardizes the future hope of peace for man throughout the globe. Unless these fundamental threats to a peaceful future are overcome, there may be little reason to concern ourselves with any other threats or social problems.

The crisis we face transcends even these grave social and political issues, and it is here that we must speak with penetrating insight. I believe, for instance, that we will find it far more difficult to bring peace to the United States than to Indochina. The depth of division and polarization in our country will never be overcome by merely finding a political solution to the Vietnam War. True reconciliation in our land will never be accomplished by mere legislative acts of Congress.

The war has not only destroyed life and limb in Indochina, it has torn our own nation apart. With each escalation of military tactics has come an intensification of bitterness, hostility, fear, and anger in America. Vindictiveness and scorn have become the common manner of both those who support and those who oppose the war. Distrust,

Mark Hatfield

hatred, and violence form a vicious cycle that threatens to engulf us all.

Added to this dilemma is the cultural revolution in our society that is completely changing the world of our young. The fundamental values of our society are being examined and challenged with increasing pressure. Our complete devotion to materialistic purposes is no longer passively accepted. Life styles are being dramatically revolutionized.

This combination of political polarization caused by the war and radical social and cultural change unveils problems that have always best been understood by the evangelical Christian. The divisiveness plaguing our land is lodged within the core of men's personalities, tied to their fears, prejudices, and insecurities.

Reconciliation among those who now hate their fellowman involves healing within each of their own lives. And the crisis of values we face as a society is really the composite of personal anguish over commitments and attitudes.

In the life, death, and resurrection of Christ we are given the only true resource for making people whole, for healing their personal wounds and bringing them into bonds of acceptance and community with all others. And through his life we are given a totally new creation—the basis for right values, attitudes, and purposes in life.

So in the midst of our contemporary cultural upheaval and social turmoil, we need to sense anew the relevance that the Good News has for both personal and corporate reconciliation.

There is today an aroused curiosity about the transcendental experience. There is a hunger for an authentic inward journey that can give us deep resources to live with hope in our age of crisis.

The Christian is one who has discovered the source of a fulfilling life that comes as a gift—God's gift through encounter with Christ. Our task—as it has always been—remains the demonstration of the validity and power of Christ's life in an age groping for such a hope.

But we must realize what we have ignored for so much of our past—that the witness of this life is never credible unless it has also embarked on an outward journey, on a mission, and given itself in love to the hurt and pain of the world in order to bring God's peace and his new creation to all men.

It is peace that we all yearn for today. Yet we know that peace is far more than can ever be negotiated at a conference or written into a treaty. It requires not only that hostility be ended but that the needs of people be fulfilled. And peace can never come perfectly among people until peace has come within them. In our day, the call to bring about such peace must be our calling. We who know something of the power and love of Jesus Christ that makes men whole and that yearns to bring together all creation must make it our calling to bring about such peace.

There are many ways in which you may choose to express your ministry in the years ahead through the opportunities which will come upon you. But in them all, I hope that you would feel compelled to be neither a Biblical Nationalist nor a Political Messiah. Rather, I hope you will apply the truth of our faith to bring peace to people, proclaiming Jesus Christ and demonstrating his relevance and love to all men in all needs, everywhere.

I trust that you will thus become an *Apostolic Peacemaker.*

Mark Hatfield

Shalom

Arnold Toynbee theorizes that nineteen out of twenty-one great civilizations deteriorated from within rather than being conquered by an external power. Today, I believe the greatest threat to our future does not come from outside the United States, but from within—from the vanishing of love and care for one another.

Likewise, the primary threat to the peace of our world stems not merely from the excessive military might which mankind possesses, but from the unmet basic human needs that plague two-thirds of the human race.

October 15, 1969, was declared "Moratorium Day" by those concerned about the continuing war in Southeast Asia. Many months before, I had accepted an invitation to speak on that same day at the "Pentagon Pulpit" program, an informal weekly gathering at noon for those who wish to hear various speakers. I thought it appropriate to keep that engagement and speak about my views on peace for our nation and our world, influenced by my experience with Christian faith. Secretary of Defense Melvin Laird, whom I know well since we attend the same church in Washington, was there and gave me a most warm and cordial welcome. The thoughts I presented had first been given in a somewhat different form to the United States Congress on Evangelism. It was a unique setting for what I had to say, in quite unusual circumstances, yet all those who were there were genuinely open to and respectful toward the ideas I expressed.

Shalom

IN DECEMBER OF 1968 I HAD the privilege of visiting India. Grave problems face that land which holds one-fifth of humanity. One particular area of the country is plagued by a small yet serious revolutionary movement—the northwestern frontier region where members of the Naga tribes have been in rebellion against the central government.

From India I went on to visit Thailand. There I became more thoroughly informed about the insurgency which threatens the northeastern section of that country. I was fascinated to learn that both of these areas had experienced the extensive influence of Christian missionaries. In my judgment, this is perhaps more than coincidental.

The Christian message of salvation includes the truth that all men are equal and valuable in God's eyes. Old customs and social mores are changed and class distinctions are done away with. The gods that entrap men into cycles of superstition, fear, and resignation to fate are destroyed. Man is offered the possibility of new life—with social and spiritual dimensions. So when societal patterns of oppression and inequity continue, isn't it plausible that revolutionary pressures claiming allegiance to human dignity and equality may be related to the influence of the Good News?

Recently I was told of an incident that made me reflect upon the impact of Christ's message and the problems of world peace. A young official in our government was relating his experiences in the Nigerian-Biafran conflict. He had been participating in negotiations to break the deadlock over relief supplies for starving elements of the Biafran population. Recently he had returned from the area after speaking with key officials from both sides as well as with those trying to administer the meager air-relief effort that is being conducted. The primary obstacle to achieving greater relief efforts, in his judgment, went beyond the tangled political, diplomatic complexities. Fundamentally, he said, the problem rested with the stubborn, unreasonable intransigence and prideful resistance that personally characterized key individual leaders on each side of the warring factions.

Shortly before leaving, my friend was discussing the relief problem with an African bishop who had major responsibility for coordinating the effort. After exploring at great length possible solutions, all of which were futile, and finding it impossible to break the political deadlock, my friend finally mentioned that some Americans were working on another approach to the situation. They were praying that the pride and selfish resistance of the key leaders might be overcome—and that they might have a change of heart and reach some reconciliation, at least on arrangements to feed innocent starving people.

The bishop at first was somewhat taken back. Having

worked for months with the political complexities of this matter, it seemed to him utterly naïve that prayer might actually be beneficial in a concrete way. But after some thought, he admitted that he would not be a bishop if he did not believe people could be changed. Faced with such a complete diplomatic impasse, prayer (as well as action) aimed at changing the personal attitudes of those involved seemed just as feasible as any other solution.

In different ways, these incidents raise provocative thoughts about evangelism and world peace; they also prompt questions about the true meaning of peace. What do we mean—and what does our faith teach—about this issue?

Some academic strategists and national security advisers avoid even speaking in terms as vague and idyllic as "world peace." Rather, they talk of increasing the probability of a world "that minimizes the incentives for armed, violent solutions to conflict situations." In other words, if there is anything one can call peace, it is the absence of war or violent conflict. This, I suspect, is the notion many of us share about the meaning of peace. It is estimated that the United States and the Soviet Union together possess explosive power equivalent to fifteen tons of TNT for every person on the earth. Yet, many postulate that such a "balance of power"—or "balance of terror," to be more precise—is the only trustworthy condition of peace.

But there is no true peace when the threat of instant annihilation hangs over the head of the majority of mankind. There is no peace when fear of destruction, rather than hope for reconciliation, is the only force restraining the use of our arsenals of nuclear devastation. I reject the simplistic notion that peace is the absence of conflict. Peace is not merely stability or order. Rather, peace is fulfillment, harmony, satisfaction, understanding, and well-being.

As long as there is deprivation, suffering, alienation, self-

Mark Hatfield

seeking, and exploitation there is no real peace. Peace can come only when needs—physical and spiritual—are fulfilled; for us, peace means far more than simply avoiding conflict. In the Old Testament, the Hebrew word for peace is *shalom*. The full meaning is actually "wholeness, soundness, completeness." Peace entails the fulfillment of needs, whether this be within a nation or within an individual. It has both a political and spiritual dimension, and an inner and outer component. A true understanding of peace includes harmony among nations, reconciliation among people, and the well-being of individuals.

Too often we speak of world peace as though it were completely unrelated to peace within nations, within communities, within families, and within individuals. It is inconsistent, for example, for a citizen to urge warring nations to make peace if he lives in hostility toward his neighbors. It seems unreasonable to protest against violence in Vietnam by employing violent tactics here at home. And it is hypocritical for a Christian to claim he has the peace of God in his heart if he remains oblivious to the violence and destruction in the world.

For a nation or an individual, peace becomes a form of relationship; it is a continuing attitude and activity, not a static condition. Fundamentally, peace is achieved by creative love—love which senses in another needs and possibilities that are not realized and seeks their fulfillment in order to create "wholeness, soundness, and completeness."

When I discuss these matters with some of my fellow Christians, they often claim that the reason we have no peace in the world is because of man's sin. As long as sin abounds, there will be "wars and rumors of wars," they say. I, of course, do not dispute the reality of man's selfish and sinful nature. But I do take issue with those who reject any responsibility for overcoming the obstacles to peace simply because sin is a reality. That was not the way of

Christ. He has not told us that evil will ultimately triumph and that we should resign ourselves to such a fate. Rather, he asks that we follow him into the midst of man's turbulent world with his reconciling and redeeming love. Recognizing the existence of sin does not eliminate our mandate to act as peacemakers.

Deprivation, suffering, hunger, alienation from God and man, lack of dignity, oppression—these strangle the world's hope for true peace. These are the obstacles to peace. True, they are perpetrated by sin—the sin of those who, absorbed by their wealth, power, privilege, and supposed self-righteousness, are blind to the responsibility of meeting these needs. Such sin is too often our own.

Christ calls us to witness to his love through our lives. That witness involves ministering to man whenever and wherever he is in need. One of the parables of our Lord provides us with valuable insights into our responsibilities as Christians. After Jesus told of the necessity to love one's neighbor, he was asked, "Who is my neighbor?" Then followed the story of the Good Samaritan in which the victim was a complete stranger to those who passed by without stopping to help, as well as to the Samaritan. The persons in this story are not individually identified; there is no indication of who it was that was robbed and injured. The point is that one's neighbor is *anyone* in need. We cannot choose our charities. When confronted with simple human need, we are called to act—and to love. As we heal wounds, we nurture peace.

We all know people who have deep personal needs—people who suffer meaninglessness, emptiness, futility, estrangement, alienation, and lack of love. These needs, when unfulfilled, will frustrate peace. They will create envy, bitterness, and discord in families and between friends; they will sustain anxiety, turmoil, and despair at the core of one's life. Here is where the obstacles to peace have their beginning—in the individual life that lacks fulfillment.

Helmut Thielicke has said: "It is possible to have Christian ideas without actually believing, and to be taken up with the social teachings of Christianity without becoming engaged personally. Then these ideas lose their connection with the Lord of Christendom and degenerate into ideologies, namely into instrumentalities of power and world mastery. Thus, it is possible for Christianity to become merely a pervasive atmosphere, a climate of social order, while faith dwindles away and the matter of *salvation* is forgotten." The love of Christ brings inner, personal peace. The gift of his Spirit is the true resource for wholeness of personality. Thus, the task of peacemaking includes the call to evangelism.

Peace, however, is also frustrated by unjust social conditions. In our communities there are people who suffer from impoverishment through no fault of their own, despite the prosperity of our land. Twenty-nine million Americans live in conditions of poverty. And although those who are nonwhite comprise only 11 percent of our population, they comprise 30 percent of the poor in our land. Millions of blacks and other minorities have been the victims of racism, have been denied dignity and justice, and are overwhelmed with hopelessness and despair. These deprivations are the power adversaries of peace. We may attempt to enforce stability, or "law and order," through the use of force; but we will never have peace in our land until we repent from this sin, correct such injustice, and fulfill these needs.

Communications have transformed our world into one neighborhood. Today, more than ever before in history, our neighbor includes anyone who lives with us on this globe. Consider the condition of our world, but, rather than looking at ourselves from a limited terrestrial perspective, let us remove ourselves from the confines of our earthly environment. Picture our planet from outside ourselves—from outer space. Look back on this blue, beautiful sphere floating through space. And then consider that the inhabitants of that planet spend fifteen times more money on creating weapons to destroy each other than on efforts to cooperate together for social and economic improvement. Yet, ten thousand of its citizens die each day because they do not have enough to eat. Two out of every three children suffer from malnutrition. Nevertheless, the average diet in one portion of that globe contains about five times more protein than the average diet of the remaining portion. Of the planet's wealth, 80 percent is controlled by only 20 percent of its inhabitants. The total wealth of those "developed" parts of this world is broken down to an average of $2,107 for each inhabitant, yet the total wealth of the remainder of the world equals only $182 for each person.

That is how we look from outside ourselves. And our Creator views his world from this perspective. As long as such an unjust distribution of the world's resources persists and continues to grow as it does at present, we can never expect to be granted true peace on earth.

A fundamental obstacle to peace, then, is the deprivation of mankind, both individually and corporately. There can be no peace within man, peace in his family, peace within our communities, and peace in the world until we fulfill the total needs of mankind. The call to evangelize is a call to proclaim and to love; it is a call to respond to these needs, and it involves us totally in the mandate of peacemaking.

Peace remains elusive as long as man continues to suffer, but peace is destroyed when one man seeks to dominate another—when men and nations seek selfish, lustful goals. We must not overlook the reality that peace is frustrated by self-assertiveness, pride, paternalism, and brutality. These are also obstacles to peace.

Living in a country that we somehow feel bears God's seal of approval, many of us tend to discover these foes of peace only in other people and nations. But Christ warns us about criticizing the speck in our brother's eye when we ignore the plank in our own. That is why it is imperative for us to examine our own policies and actions in the world to understand how they may inhibit the prospects for lasting peace.

Why should we, a nation founded by those seeking a new world blessed by God, now be bound by "an eye for an eye, a tooth for a tooth"?

For individuals as well as nations, needs cannot be fulfilled and peace cannot be experienced until men and nations repent, receive forgiveness, and become reconciled.

We must always remember that regardless of the circumstances the world is in, history remains under God's sovereignty. In Ephesians Paul writes that God "purposes in his sovereign will that all human history shall be consummated in Christ, that everything that exists in Heaven or earth shall find its perfection and fulfillment in him" (Eph. 1:9-10, Phillips).

God's entrance into history through Christ has revolutionary implications for our attitudes toward our fellowman. Again in Ephesians we read: "He has made a unity of the conflicting elements of Jew and Gentile by breaking down the barrier which lay between us. . . . and made in himself out of the two, Jew and Gentile, one new man, thus producing peace. For he reconciled both to God by the sacrifice of one body on the cross, and by this act made utterly irrelevant the antagonism between them. Then he came and told both you who were far from God and us who were near that the war was over" (Eph. 2:14-17, Phillips).

In God's eyes, then, every person is of infinite value. God does not judge people as Americans or Russians or Chinese. He does not categorize them according to nationalistic, political, or ideological labels. Christ has broken through those barriers. God views each person as his unique creation—so valuable that he gave his son for each of them. God's purpose is to bring all creation into unity through Christ.

In the Old Testament, the vision of God's final peace is clear. In both Isaiah and Micah, for example, we are told of the day when nations "shall beat their swords into plowshares, and their spears into pruning hooks; nation shall not lift up sword against nation, neither shall they learn war any more" (Isa. 2:4, Mic. 4:3, RSV). God's strategy is to bring this to pass; we do not know the time, but we know that he controls history and is moving it toward this end. It is true that formidable adversaries face the realization of God's peace and purpose in the world: "For we wrestle not against flesh and blood, but against principalities, against powers, against the rulers of the darkness" (Eph. 6:12). Yet we know that God's power, which raised Christ from the dead, has put him at "a place that is infinitely superior to any conceivable command, authority, power or control, and which carries with it a name far beyond any name that could ever be used in this world or the world to come. God has placed everything under the power of Christ . . ." (Eph. 1:21–22, Phillips). We will find trouble and turmoil in the world, yet we know that Christ has overcome the world.

Our responsibility is to bear witness to the love of God through Christ. This is a mission of peace, and we are under the call of God to fulfill it. In this task we must not be bound by rigid categories of what is a spiritual message and what is a social action. We cannot build a barrier between theological issues and social questions. We must not make the mistake of believing that the Good News we proclaim has no relevance to our attitudes and actions toward political as well as personal problems in our homes, our

Mark Hatfield

nation, and our world. For too long the artificial polarization between those who preach the truth of individual conversion and the activists who proclaim some form of a "social gospel" has prohibited a full understanding of the gospel's meaning in our world. Christ calls us to express his love through all that we do. We are to meet the needs of others—spiritual and physical. Whether we are relating to one another the reality of Christ's life or giving a cup of cold water in his name, we are bearing witness to that love.

Our task requires personal involvement in the world. We cannot abdicate our personal responsibility to an institutional response. Unfortunately, our tendency is to seek escape from personal involvement in problems confronting us by endorsing institutional solutions to them. We give money to the church's missionary fund, we donate clothes to the street mission, and we contribute faithfully to worthy causes, believing that these are the only avenues through which we can carry out God's work. Yet, what is most needed is individual, personal involvement. We must make our lives relevant to others; we must involve ourselves personally in situations where we demonstrate the concern and compassion Christ imparts to us. We must engage ourselves personally in sharing with others our experience of God's love.

Just as our religious institutions cannot become a substitute for our personal responsibility to minister to human needs, they also cannot provide any insulated shelter from the trauma of the world. The church was never meant to be a fortress that protected its members from the perils of the outside world. Rather, the church is those believers who gather to strengthen and encourage one another for their involvement in the world. That task, of course, includes churchly responsibilities of preaching, edifying, and instructing. But evangelism—our message and mission as Christians—is primarily an individual rather than an institutional responsibility.

At what point does this responsibility for carrying forth the message of Christ's life and earnestly seeking God's peace for the world become relevant in each of our lives? What is it that we can do?

Our faith calls us to seek God's will for man and for the world. We must look at our own country, examine the values that are guiding our culture, and ask whether they are true to God's will and purpose. If not, they must be challenged with a prophetic word, and Christians must witness to the need for national repentance—that is, the need to turn from present ways "unto the way of the Lord."

In our democracy, the values and commitments of the nation rest fundamentally with the people. The corporate effect of the people's thoughts and actions eventually influences the shape of our society. As Christians, our basic responsibility is to express the values and truths that we have acquired through our faith. Further, we must attempt to implant them within the lives of others. Therefore, one of the urgent avenues for personal action is to influence public attitudes and values. Public opinion drove a president out of office in 1968; the attitudes of the people in our democracy can change the course of our country.

So we must be diligent and responsible in the expression of our views regarding the state of our nation. We must attempt to mold public attitudes so they will become attuned to God's purposes. The leaven of the kingdom of God must continually make its entry into the life of our nation; it can do so only through the witness of our lives.

When we look at the state of our nation, how should we react? What should our attitude be toward a people who are absorbed by materialism, controlled by greed, and motivated by the pursuit of selfish and corporate gain, with little regard to the value and quality of human life? How should we judge the way our nation uses its resources? We are all called to be stewards of those resources. Are we, as a nation, utilizing our abundance in a way that pleases

God and attempts to seek his purposes for mankind?

When we conclude that our nation is not following God's way, then we must speak out. That must be part of our witness. And that is where each of us can take personal responsibility.

Ancient Israel experienced situations similar to those of our own land. In their quest for stability and power, the Hebrew people were often tempted to trust in their military power as the ultimate source of security. Hosea warned prophetically against this danger: "Because you have trusted in your chariots and in the multitude of your warriors, therefore the tumult of war shall arise among your people" (Hos. 10:13–14, RSV).

The question is not whether we should have an army, but rather, whether our trust rests solely in our military power as a means of insuring our security and peace. The Scripture does not condone such a trust.

You and I are confronted personally with this issue. Where is our trust? Do we believe that our military might is the final guarantee of peace? Does our personal trust fundamentally rest in chariots and warriors, or do we really believe peace is a gift granted by God and not a utopia insured by armed might? Our individual convictions on this matter, as Christians and citizens, will have an effect on our nation's destiny.

Our point of individual involvement, then, begins with an evaluation of our own attitudes and values concerning the Christian commission to seek peace. We must look within ourselves and see if we truly possess God's inner peace. We must look to our families, to those close to us, and ask if we are pursuing God's peace in all these relationships. We must look to our communities: what are we doing about the frustrated needs of many who inhabit them? We must look to our country: are we as a people truly seeking God's path to peace? How are we involved in speaking forth our convictions and causing our nation to change its course? Finally, we must look to the world: what have we done to alleviate the human misery and cultural chasms that destroy the foundations of any lasting peace?

Our personal involvement must be characterized by an examination of our own thinking in light of God's purposes, by relevant action to bring peace to those situations of conflict that touch our lives, and by the proclamation of God's redemptive love.

Changes in people will have to occur if we are to discover any true peace. People must permit God to transform their values, their attitudes, and their purpose in life. This, in part, is the meaning of conversion. The individual who becomes oriented to the person of Christ is radically re-created. He is no longer in complete bondage to his selfish goals. The focus of his life is in seeking to do God's will. God's Spirit injects new life—Christ's life. Thus, values, attitudes, and purposes become reformulated. The world is visualized through its Creator's perspective, and his peace is sought.

The mission of peace cannot be severed from the task of evangelism. Seeking peace requires witnessing to God's will, judging nations, orienting one's life to the purposes of his peace, influencing the thinking of the public, acting in love towards our neighbors, and proclaiming the power of God to remake human life according to the "fullness of Christ."

Today our situation is much like that which confronted the primitive church. As a small band, the first Christians faced a pagan world. But they did not choose to remain in Jerusalem, fortifying themselves against their enemies. They became the church dispersed, the church on mission. Brave, small bands infiltrated all levels of society throughout the known world. The impact was revolutionary,

Mark Hatfield

changing the entire course of civilization as the message of Christ's life spread throughout the Roman Empire.

Today we also must leave our institutional seclusion and go forth into the midst of the world's suffering and turmoil. We go with love to bring peace. We cannot be bound by our institutions, our organizations, and our comforts—all those things that serve as spiritual security blankets. We must seek to bring fulfillment to every need, to bring peace to every conflict.

Peace will not come to earth until the total needs of mankind are met. Changed lives must implement the mission of peace through the changing of society.

We cannot protect the status quo. Peace is not static. The Christian must realize that the impact of his message challenges and questions things as they are and claims that new life is possible.

So we go forth into the world seeing new possibilities, grasping God's vision of what he can do. We have the certain hope that he can impart new life—new life to individuals, to nations, and to all creation. That hope is based in the Risen Christ. All history is consummated in him. He is our Peace.

Out of Seclusion

*The challenge to the Christian church is
not to preserve its religious establishment
per se. That should be plainly evident from
the words and witness of Christ's own life. He
was straightforward in his condemnation of
scribes and Pharisees—those who were too
concerned over their appearance of piety. He
minced no words in rebuking those who loved to
sit in the front seats at church and who said
their prayers loudly in public as demonstrations
of their righteousness. Christ warned that such
outward pretension only further demonstrated
the necessity for inner repentance. He looked for
practice rather than pious rhetoric.
Much of our religious establishment today
needs to hear again the whole truth of Christ's
message. With the serious issues of war, race,
hunger, and poverty impinging upon us, the
Christian must follow Christ in deeds as well as
in words. These thoughts pressed upon me with
particular force, and I tried to articulate them
when I was invited to address the Southern
Baptist Convention in 1967.*

Out of Seclusion

THE GREAT COMMISSION OF Jesus Christ to his disciples and to his church was threefold. First of all he said, "Go teach all nations." The second part of that commission was, "Baptize them in the name of the Father, and of the Son and of the Holy Spirit." The third part was, "Teach them to observe all things whatsoever I have commanded you." And then he promised to be with us always, even to the end of the world.

I believe the Scriptures are very clear as to what Christ meant by that third part. Yet this is the aspect of our mission which we most often fail to accomplish.

Let us take, for example, the very important matter of Christ's dealing with human suffering and need. The actions of Christ, as recorded in the Gospels, offer vivid examples of the fact that God does not intend for human beings to suffer endlessly under the pressures of poverty, hunger, social decay, racial persecution, disease, ignorance, unemployment, war, or violence.

The major part of Christ's public ministry on earth was spent in the healing of human suffering, in alleviating the sickness and social deprivation of mankind. Christ *did* heal the sick, raise the dead, cleanse the leper, feed the multitudes. He gave purpose to the wandering, sight to the blind, forgiveness to the repentant. Then he said, "Greater things than I have done, you shall do. Keep my commandments, if you love me" (John 14:12, 15).

I believe that there has developed within the church a spirit of withdrawal from the world, a secure seclusion in noninvolvement. Some people have left the church spiritually to join in the task of using the powers of the state to create a perfect world and to legislate virtue. They have cared for man's social and temporal needs. Others have taken a suspicious look at these advocates of the social gospel and have decided not to become involved in the worldly affairs of man. They have tended only to the soul and to the defense of theology. Both groups are forgetting the example of Christ.

The Christians in this country and especially in the mission fields throughout the entire world have done a very creditable job of pioneering in social concern for suffering mankind. We dare not forget the loving sacrifice of Christian men and women who have sought to rescue the souls, the minds, the bodies of men in every nation of the world. But today we see missionary doors closed. Certain countries have said to missionaries in all churches of the Christian faith, "No longer are you permitted to come to our land to preach this gospel." Fortunately, we have found that where the missionaries have created an indigenous, native church and leadership, the removal of the missionaries has not resulted in the cessation of the Christian church. Rather, these people who have learned a sense of independence have stood on their own feet and have re-mained faithful to the church. They have been committed to a cause, to a person, and they have been willing to make sacrifices for what they believe. Very clearly—regardless of our political label, regardless of our political philosophy, regardless of our religious persuasion—men who are in need are men whom we have a responsibility to assist. Yet, we must remember that ultimately we cannot do for others that which they are not willing to do for themselves.

John Foster Dulles and John F. Kennedy very eloquently translated this into the world of international politics when they said, "You cannot superimpose the cause of freedom upon another man unless he is willing to fight and die for it himself."

This is why some of us are concerned that in Southeast Asia we are involved in a conflict that is calling on us to do for the Asians that which they should be doing or at least be willing to do for themselves. We have committed more and more American boys at the same time that the South Vietnamese forces continue to desert their own cause. Now we have taken over the pacification program. We ask the question, "Why?" Today our boys are called upon to fight other nations' wars. But why are not the words of President Johnson—which were so plainly stated in 1964—just as true today as they were then when he said to the American people, "This is an Asian war that must be fought by Asian boys." Are we not being asked to do for other people what they are not willing to do for themselves?

We must be willing to aid the cause of freedom and of mankind throughout the entire world. That's our role in world leadership. But let us not forget that the United States of America does have limitations on her resources, both manpower and material resources. We cannot become world policemen and dissipate our resources wherever a crisis occurs. Our nation must hear a voice of the people that says to our government, "We want to uphold our responsibilities but we believe we have an obligation to use our creative genius to find alternatives to war, alternatives that will not consign our youth, our greatest national resource, to an endless conflict that has been going on for twenty years." And, we are told it may go on yet another two, ten, or twenty years.

It is these kinds of questions that we must raise today, in Christian concern; not that we are all going to agree on the answers. But we should ask today as Christians and as Americans for guidelines, accurate information, facts upon which we can depend and make our judgments and our evaluations. I believe, therefore, that as Christians, we must be involved in these great issues and not abdicate them to diplomats or to military generals. This is a responsibility of *all* of the citizens of this nation.

We should have a great concern as Christians today for man's physical well-being. A recent magazine ad stated that if the hungry of the earth were lined up at your door, they would encircle the world forty-five times. Jesus Christ said, "Feed my sheep." I believe that people who have never seen hunger cannot truly imagine its horror.

In 1945 the part of the United States Navy in which I was serving was ordered into Indochina. We were to pick up part of Chiang Kai-shek's Nationalist Army and carry it up into Northern China to fight the Chinese Communists. I recall that as we went into Haiphong port that early morning we could see the Chinese troops lined up on the beach ready to move aboard our ships. We could see the sacks of rice they had brought with them to be their food supply. As each sack was lifted from the beach, Vietnamese women scratched around in the sand hoping to find a few kernels of rice that had sifted through the burlap bags. As we drove into the city of Hanoi, we saw dead Vietnamese—dead not

Conflict and Conscience   **56**

because of bullet wounds, but because of starvation.

I believe that the problem of hunger will shape the destiny of more nations and their political philosophies than any other force in the world today. Most of us in America, the well-fed part of the world, cannot comprehend this. In most instances the missionary can. And many churchmen who have been close to that missionary understand. But do you realize that in many parts of the world people spend four-fifths of their annual income of $100 just for food? Many of us in America spend more than that to keep our pets alive and well-fed. Our own agricultural progress has tended to make us oblivious to the hunger in the rest of the world.

What has happened? *Has* the church failed in its mission? *Has* the church lost its impetus to help troubled and hungry people? By his example, Christ told us to care, to sacrifice, to use our resources for the service of others. But have we obeyed? Do we assume the responsibility to meet the needs of the whole community in which we live and even of the world, of which we are a part?

On the one side stands God with his abundant resources and his command for social concern. On the other side is the need of the world and of each individual man. The Christian is supposed to be the minister of reconciliation between the two sides, bringing together God's resources and man's need. The Christian is to be the instrument for the total solution of the problem.

But all too often when people go to church seeking meaning for their lives, they are offered a cup of coffee rather than a demand upon conscience. The church has been rendering unto Caesar its role of concern for people. We might edit the story of the Good Samaritan a bit to make him the man today who votes to give other peoples' money to anybody left hurt along the wayside. Or, as one Kentucky lawyer said, "We Christianized the federal govern-

ment because we would not tithe to do the job ourselves."
Too many Christians have no twinge of conscience when
they pass the sick man on the road. We rationalize that we
have paid the Good Samaritan to come along after us to
take care of this rather unpleasant social obligation.

Unfortunately, the average person in church today is
frequently left with an incomplete Christian experience.
By abdication of its concern for others, by deliberate dele-
gation of its Good Samaritan responsibility, the church in
effect leads its members into the sin of self-concern. People
are invited to use the church only for self-improvement
rather than as a place of service.

In reality the Christian should be the best qualified and
the most able to relieve human suffering and to change the
world in which he lives. Actually no other culture or religious background has given birth to social progress equal
to that made in Christian lands. Why is this? The theology
of the Christian faith, I believe, releases the creative energies of man for his life here on earth.

Many religions are oriented only toward preparing man
for the life hereafter. They try to negate man's life here on
earth and point to the release from suffering which will
come only after death. But there is never the security, the
assurance in these religions that guarantees life after death.
The tension of this insecurity keeps the followers of these
religions oriented to the mystery of the other world.

But look at Christianity. The resurrection of Jesus Christ
from the dead guarantees our life after death. God has
given us victory over death and fear of what lies beyond
the grave. Our faith, then, is secure. Our eternal destiny is
established. So now, because of this truth and because of
the love-dynamic of Christ, we can turn our efforts and
our creative energies to the revolutionizing of our world—
to the alleviating of human suffering and to the work of
God on earth. This is the potential. But we have fallen

short. We have painted Jesus Christ as a respectable, sub-urban, stand-pat establishmentarian, defending the status quo, instead of recognizing him as the greatest political, social, economic, and spiritual revolutionary the world has ever known.

And so today we find that some of the people most criti-cal of the government's welfare and poverty programs often are the evangelical Christians. Yet all of these criti-cisms are made from the safety of our churches, isolated many times from the social needs of our world. We point the accusing finger at the government, at the war on pov-erty, at the social gospeler; but many times we refuse to obey the mandate of Christ to heal, to redeem, to feed, and to nourish the spirit, to cleanse and uplift, to educate and change the heart, to house and clothe, and to share the love of Christ.

If the church had been doing the job it was called to do, a job which only it can do rightly, there would be no need for the government to enter the picture.

It is high time for the church to obey her Lord and as-sume the task of meeting the social needs of the world in the love and power of Christ. Let me give you an example of what could be done with a pressing domestic problem. The hard-core unemployable segment of our population in America totals about one million. We have in America today over 300,000 church congregations. If each congre-gation would take responsibility for three persons in this group of unemployables, we could see that a huge govern-ment welfare program for the unemployed would not be necessary.

In my opinion, this is the great challenge and the call of the Christian church today: to go out and identify with human need and become involved in the completion of the commission—"to observe all things whatsoever I have commanded you." For we know that in training a man for a new job, he can also be shown a new purpose in life—as we heal his body, we can point to the healing of his spirit. And when we feed a person, the way is open to minister to the spiritual hunger in his heart.

And, if at times the job seems impossible and we become discouraged, we can take heart in the amazing words of Jesus: "And greater things than I have done, you shall do."

The (Holy?)
Spirit of '76

In the midst of our contemporary social turmoil and sense of national crisis, we tend to forget that our nation was born out of a revolutionary spirit. Further, that spirit was molded by the deep religious motivation and spiritual vision that moved those who settled our land.

When I was invited to be one of the speakers at a conference on American heritage held at John Brown University, I chose to stress these themes. I remain convinced that recovering the prayer perspective of our past can provide us with the needed vision today to shape our future destiny.

The (Holy?) Spirit of '76

CONTEMPORARY AMERICA finds itself in a century which future historians may characterize as the "Age of Revolution." This century was born with the political and economic revolution of the Soviet Union—its civilities have been threatened by the counterrevolutions of nazism and fascism. Empires have been destroyed through national revolutions during the twentieth century, and established forms of knowledge, social organization, and ethical expression have been challenged by science and technology, transportation and communication, skepticism and nihilism.

Until recently, much of the revolutionary ferment of the twentieth century had either passed us by or affected us only indirectly. The Soviet revolution was, after all, a European revolt against a feudal order the likes of which never existed on the American continent. And the barbarities of the Nazis and the Fascists did not evoke our collective response until we ourselves were forced through self-defense to join the war effort. The impact of technology and modern economic organization was softened by the opportunities provided by the ever-new frontiers to the West. The philosophical and intellectual crisis of Western civilization was muted by the pragmatic and nontheoretical character of the American people.

It is only recently that we have become aware that we cannot hide forever behind the barriers which have isolated us from these realities. Technology has forced us to look across the oceans. Modern economic organization has involved us deeply not only with the developed nations but with the Third World countries of Africa and Asia. And the confrontation with radically new situations and ideas contrary to our own traditions and beliefs can no longer be settled on the simple grounds of pragmatism alone.

Evidence that we are no longer isolated from the revolutionary movements of our century surrounds each of us every day. Radicals have questioned the validity of our political system, theologians have questioned the integrity of our religious beliefs, minorities have questioned the authority of government by majority rule; and students have questioned the goodness of our national goals at home and abroad. We are a divided country: divided by race, divided by age, divided by region, and divided by belief.

It is, perhaps, somewhat ironic that I should begin by pointing out that the heritage of America is itself being questioned by revolutionaries at home and abroad. Both our democratic institutions and the moral basis of our civilization are in a time of crisis, and it hardly seems appropriate that we should spend our time talking about the past. After all, many people are now saying that it is no longer a question as to *whether* America will undergo a revolution, but only as to *what type* of revolution it will be.

It is my thesis, however, that a proper understanding of our heritage is a tool which may be used both to understand and to help shape the changes which are pressing upon us in the present and which will continue to force themselves upon us in the future. Indeed, to know our American heritage is to realize that it bears within itself a remarkable capacity for renewal and reform. Our nation was born in revolution. It was born of pioneers who attempted to form a new type of community in a new world. It is not by chance that we were referred to by European countries as the New World, or that our settlements were referred to as New England, or that our largest city bears the name New York. It is not by chance that our currency has inscribed upon it the words *novus ordo seclorum* (a new order for the ages). It is not by chance that the first "political groundbreaking" took place in the city of Philadelphia—the city of brotherly love.

America was a land of new beginnings where the ills of an old and dying order could be left behind. One historian described the Puritan settlements as a bold and energetically sustained effort "to put into operation a utopian commonwealth."

Why is it, then, that we have suddenly become so fearful of change? One of the reasons, I believe, is that we have forgotten the revolutionary implications of our own heritage. And if we are to be once again the nation of vision and dreams, of human renewal and institutional reform, we must again become sensitive to our own heritage.

I have already referred to my belief that the American heritage has a strain of revolutionary fervor that equips us with the ability for reform and self-renewal. One more thing which I would like to stress is that the American heritage was profoundly religious. It was religious inspiration and vision which provided much of the dynamic energy assuring the success of the American spirit. It was

Mark Hatfield

the religious factor which placed guidelines and limitations on American revolutionary fervor. And if we are to recapture the dynamic of our earlier years as a nation, we must also recover the religious sense which gave direction and stability to the changes which were wrought out of the new order.

I realize, of course, that to speak of revolution can be dangerous and misleading. I realize even more that to link religious fervor with revolutionary commitment can be one of the most dangerous options available to mankind. After all, the totalitarianisms of the twentieth century have been inspired by secularized religious fervor; I believe, however, that the American experience has within it checks and balances which would place guidelines on the nature and methods of revolutionary change itself. It is to that heritage which I should now like to direct myself.

The inspiration of America is largely religious. Our earliest settlers came to this continent having fled religious persecution both in England and in the Netherlands. The religious basis of our society was often noticed by European writers who visited our country. De Tocqueville in his *Democracy in America* wrote a century ago:

> It must never be forgotten that religion gave birth to Anglo-American society. In the United States, religion is therefore mingled with all the habits of the nation and all the feelings of patriotism, whence it derives a peculiar force.[1]

Pre–Civil War English travelers were amazed that although the United States was still a rather primitive country, there were as many churches in America as there were in the British Isles. Because they observed an almost continuous succession of religious assemblages and were confronted by the fact that large donations were constantly being made for religious purposes, they concluded that America was basically a very religious country.

Social scientists tell us that the Puritan ethic played a significant role in the early success of the nation's economic life. Likewise, political scientists demonstrate easily the relationship between Protestant theology which questioned the moral purity of all humanity and the institutions of limited government with divided powers and checks and balances. James Madison declared: "The accumulations of all powers, legislative, executive, and judiciary, by the same hands, whether of one, a few, or many, and whether heredi- tary, self-appointive, or elective, may justly be pronounced the very definition of tyranny." [2]

Even our separation of church and state comes to us not out of a desire to create a secular society, but through the effort to insure the integrity of religious expression. Further, it not only prevented the state from enforcing religious belief, but it kept the church from giving religious sanction to the acts of the state.

Not only did our religious heritage inspire the founding of a new nation in a new world, contribute to the economic vitality of the national enterprise, help formulate our con- cepts of limited government, and contribute to our doc- trines of civil rights and free expression, but it also dealt with the very rights of man himself. In a world which heretofore had been based on class orders, our religious heritage proclaimed that all men were created equal in the sight of God. And almost a hundred years before the British—under the influence of the great Christian states- man William Wilberforce—the early Americans questioned the age-old practice of slavery which until this time had been nothing more than an assumption that all the great powers of past history had taken for granted.

I believe the early success of the American experiment is an example of the biblical injunction, "Seek ye first the kingdom of God, and all these things shall be added unto you." Those who came to this country were not preoccupied with the amassing of wealth or with building a great nation-state. Rather, their chief concern was founding a society upon the laws and commands of God. John Cotton, minister to the Massachusetts Bay Colony, stated, "Purity, preserved in the church, will preserve well-ordered liberty in the people, and both of them establish well-balanced authority in the magistrates." [3] Another Puritan spokesman, John Higginson, declared:

> My fathers and brethren, this is never to be forgotten that New England is originally a plantation of religion not a plantation of trade. Let merchants and such as are increasing cent per cent remember this, that worldly gain was not the end and design of the people of New England.[4]

As the colonies met with political and economic success, the religious base of the society gradually weakened. Instead of recognizing that the truths of religion supplied the dynamism and social cohesiveness which brought about the success of the American experiment, they began to seek their success in so-called laws of economics and government. Thus, the success of an individualistic and capitalist economy began to be worshiped as a thing in itself rather than as an expression of the biblical concept that as a man works, so shall he prosper.

The mistaking of a particular form of this expression, as opposed to its broader meaning that work is an order sanctioned by God and the means by which he is to earn his livelihood, led to the sanctification of the economic concept itself. This could be tolerated so long as an expanding frontier and a relatively open economy allowed virtually all people to make an honorable living. But as the frontier was conquered and the economy became more sophisticated, there were literally millions on this continent who were frozen out of the economy. There were those whose work was exploited, and there were those who could find no work at all. The religious basis of our early economy was exploited as a rationalization for the status quo. In time, even the religious heritage itself was denied, and a social Darwinism appeared which argued that the laws of nature dictated that only the fittest should survive—that the suffering and poverty of millions was the natural expression of God-ordained laws governing the economic and social affairs of mankind.

Likewise, in the area of political theory, the concept of limited government—originally based on a biblically derived distrust of power under the cognizance that all men were fallen creatures subject to greed and lust—became absolutized at the expense of those who had no hope but to turn to government for their protection against the concentrated power of modern economic organization.

Thus, while the religious basis of American society originally served as the cultural dynamic which helped assure its success, in later years it was perverted and used as a rationalization for the self-interests of those who were comfortable under the existing situation. And so, one commentator in the nineteenth century stated:

> Man cannot interfere with His work without marring it. The attempts of legislators to turn the industry of society in one direction or another, out of its natural and self-chosen channels—here to encourage it by bounties, and there to load it with penalties—to increase or diminish the supply of the market, to establish a maximum of price, to keep specie in the country—are almost invariably productive of harm. *Laissez faire;* "these things regulate themselves," in common phrase; which means, of course, that God regulates them by His general laws, which always, in the long run, work to good.[5]

While only 150 years earlier the Puritans were stressing that the basis of our society was a religious one, we had

　　　　　　　　　　　　　　　Mark Hatfield

come instead to worship business and the rights of property. In 1886, *The Nation* editorialized:

> The popular hero today . . . is neither the saint, the sage, the scholar, the soldier, nor the statesman, but the successful stockgambler. . . . And what is worst of all, there is growing tendency to believe that everybody is entitled to whatever he can buy, from the Presidency down to a street-railroad franchise.[6]

Gradually, much of the institutional church in America began to give its official sanction to the rights of property and business as opposed to the more fundamental rights of freedom and human dignity. Religion was used, unfortunately, as a mask to cover the worst of our corporate ills. Pierre Berton, a Canadian writer of some repute, was asked by the Anglican Church of Canada to describe the reasons why he left the church and Christianity. He gave those reasons in a book entitled *The Comfortable Pew* which quickly became a best seller. One of Berton's chief complaints against the church is that it has in fact forgotten its ministry to the needy and less fortunate, that in fact it has forsaken its own values in exchange for the popular values of the community. Berton argues:

> It has all but been forgotten that Christianity began as a revolutionary religion whose followers embraced an entirely different set of values from those held by other members of society. Those original values are still in conflict with the values of contemporary society; yet religion today has become as conservative a force as the force the original Christians were in conflict with.[7]

When Robert and Helen Lynd, two great American sociologists, did their famous study concerning life in an average American town, they concluded that religion's role was "not to raise troublesome questions and to force attention to disparities between values and current practice." In their own words, the Lynds stated that religion in Middletown had become "an emotionally stabilizing agent." [8]

Is it any wonder then that there are indications coming from many fronts that religion is rapidly losing strength in our society? For what can religion offer us if it serves nothing more than to confirm our establishmentarian prejudices? In 1968, the Gallup Poll asked the question, "At the present time, do you think religion as a whole is increasing its influence on American life, or losing its influence?" Of those who gave an opinion, 18 percent thought that religion was increasing its influence while 67 percent felt that religion was losing its influence. Those who thought religion was losing influence outnumbered the others by almost four to one! [9]

This present relationship between the church and pressing social problems here in America disturbs me greatly. For one thing, it tends to keep people whom we might expect to have the highest motivations and the purest concern from becoming actively involved in these problems. The quest for a just social order thus becomes purely secular, and the religious dimension of poverty—the poverty of the human spirit—is neglected while material dimensions of poverty are attacked. The saints of the present are, in the words of Albert Camus, "secular saints."

I tend to disagree with this whole concept of "secular sainthood," for I feel that only the genuinely religious dimension of concern for our fellow-man can overcome the self-interest which characterizes virtually all political activity. But the truth of the matter is that concerned people seem to find little or no support in their churches in the quest they are making for a more just social order. If the church does not want the new order to be purely a secular order—or more important, if the church believes that a

Mark Hatfield

secular order is not genuinely possible, that all social and political order ultimately rests on religious and philosophical values—it had better reexamine its relationship to the forces for social justice and betterment in this country and throughout the world.

My concern over this problem is not only my concern for the church, it is also for the character of the changes which are going to make themselves felt in our country one way or another, like it or not. I am not only convinced that a church which divorces itself from the movement toward social justice will become irrelevant to the needs of modern society, I am also convinced that any movement toward social justice will be illusory if it cannot be related to the ultimate question of human dignity and freedom—the relationship between man and God. Once any revolutionary movement becomes devoid of this ultimate concern, it tends to degenerate into authoritarianism and totalitarianism. Further, only the strength of religious vision and dedication can maintain the commitment necessary to achieve the goals which need our national attention. And if the religious community is unable to provide that motivation, it will have to come from a secular ideology with all the dangers that implies.

I do not wish to be misunderstood, however, concerning the role of the church, as I see it, in the social sector. I do not believe that the church as an institution should attempt an active role in policy decisions of government. For, once those decisions were made, the church would then be in a position of having to sanction the government itself as being holy and just. But the church does have the obligation to mobilize its own members and communicants to an awareness of the dimensions of the problems around them and to spread the message that in serving man we are also serving the God who told us to love our neighbors as ourselves.

Conflict and Conscience

Too often Christians have allowed the concept of universal sin and the fallen man to interfere with any attempt at social reform. But, we must never forget that in Jesus Christ all history has been touched by the hand of God as well as by the sin of man.

One Christian gentleman who is very concerned over this problem has written recently:

> The quest for human values in our society, one must say at the beginning, has been radically secularized. It has moved outside the churches. If one wishes to be radically religious in our society—that is to say, radically committed to a vision of human brotherhood, personal integrity, openness to the future, justice, and peace—one will not, commonly, seek an ecclesiastical outlet for one's energies. One will, instead, find community under secular auspices, create one's own symbols for community and integrity, and work through secular agencies for social and political reforms. The saints of the present (and perhaps of the future) are no longer ecclesiastics or churchgoers, or even, necessarily, believers in God.[10]

I would not urge you to accept the fallacies so often uttered in American political debate that by improving a man's environment we can improve man himself. But I would urge you to support the causes of social progress because many of them are right in themselves. A minimum wage will not make a person less sinful, but a man has the right nonetheless to fair compensation for his labor. Government cannot legislate love among the races, but all men have a right to share in our respect and affection equally on the basis of their equality before the Creator.

I believe that the church must open its eyes to the vision of a better society, or else it will by default share in the guilt for the nightmare of a secular ideological totalitarianism. We need men of vision who have the courage to sail

Mark Hatfield

across the North Atlantics of the twentieth century and propound the religious basis of a new order for this nation —an order that will take into account not only fallen man, but the question of what God wants this man to be.

Nothing could be more true to the American heritage. Nothing could be more necessary to the preservation of the American heritage.

To Heal the World

I have a great deal of respect for the evangelical outreach of many Christian denominations, particularly those who spread the balm of God's love in the healing ministry of medicine. In February 1970, I was invited to address the Alumni Postgraduate Convention of Loma Linda University in Southern California. Since I was to be addressing mostly doctors and nurses who had been trained by or were in training at Loma Linda, I decided to talk to them about some of the new challenges to medicine in foreign fields and the need for an emphasis on proper nutrition of the poor both at home and abroad, tying in this theme with the injunction of Jesus Christ to bind up the wounds of the world and to feed his sheep.

Loma Linda University is a training ground for many doctors who serve in Seventh Day Adventist hospitals overseas. Their medical mission is truly inspiring, and it was a tremendously moving experience for me to share ideas with this particular audience.

To Heal the World

Enganld's late great Prime Minister Benjamin Disraeli once observed that the economic health of a nation is based first on the health of her people. This has greater relevance today than Disraeli ever dreamed of at the height of the British Empire.

Improved physical well-being must be reckoned with as an important factor in a nation's ability to develop, to grow, to prosper, and to attain economic viability and political stability.

A healthy population contributes to and forms the basic ingredients for an economically healthy and progressive nation. And nowhere is this observation better proved than in the problems of hungry societies.

The International Conference on Protein Malnutrition held in 1964 concluded that "the most prominent deterrent to progress in developing countries is the failure of healthful developments of pre-school children resulting from malnutrition."

Infants and children require a balanced nutritional intake of protein, carbohydrate, and fat if they are to enjoy a mentally prosperous adult life with the intellect developed to its fullest potential.

Balanced dietary intake for adults is equally essential for the prolonged gainful labor that develops a country. One cannot expect, for instance, a 3,500-calorie output of labor from an intake of less than 2000 calories, the majority of which is carbohydrates.

John Montgomery in his book *Foreign Aid in International Politics* emphasizes this point: "It is now a truism to observe that the basic obstacles to growth are non-economic. Illiteracy, lack of technical and managerial skills, social injustice, inadequate public administration and vagueness of national will cannot be eliminated by economic aid alone." [1]

I am well aware that developing the full human potential is extraordinarily difficult and a very slow, painful undertaking. It must be done, however, if developing nations are to become capable of putting to use the technical know-how available to them and if they are to raise permanently the standard of living of their people.

But, how do we develop human resources?

I know of only one way.

We need more direct, personal aid to the people of developing countries. We cannot educate people merely by sending them books or money. We cannot eliminate disease by sending only medical supplies or money. The development of human potential requires person-to-person contact.

Some primitive peoples are still living at a fifteenth-century level. They must be taught the importance of medicine—indeed, even simple hygiene—before they can make good use of medical supplies. A number of such humanitarian programs of direct assistance to the people of developing nations already exist.

Christ's mission was to a wounded world. And the pages of the New Testament are filled with instances of his healing ministry. Surely we are his hands in this world-wide mission of bringing a restoration of health to suffering mankind.

But, even though much has been done, there is more to do.

As industry becomes computerized—with more factories such as those in Detroit making cylinder blocks in which there are only machines, no humans—we will all have more time to give to this task of binding up the wounds of hungry and suffering mankind.

Those who have been warning about the coming world famine are becoming less insistent this year, as evidence of the possibilities of a "green revolution" arise to give man hope. Man may yet make it, in spite of contrary predictions, if we turn our attention to man and his needs instead of to the excessive production of weapons of war.

You are aware, I am sure, of the new strain of rice which has been grown in Vietnam and produces three crops a year instead of one. This is being grown in the Philippines as well, and other rice-producing peoples are, with American help, experimenting with it.

India, with increasing use of American help and know-how, is using American fertilizers with the resultant increase of food for her hungry masses. There may be hope that India will become self-sustaining in the production of food.

But there is more to do. The plight of starving Biafra touched all our hearts. The West poured out its food for the starving people and will continue to do so. Who can forget the pictures of little children, their bellies swollen by the *hunger-produced* disease kwashiorkor—a lack of protein severe enough to cause death?

American technological know-how could provide the means to enrich *all* its grains with enzyme proteins (as has

Mark Hatfield

been done with protein-deficient wheat sent to India). American companies are already producing protein-enriched beverages for sale in some countries and this could be expanded.

Doctors in the United States, by and large, have neglected the important study of nutrition simply because the crippling diseases of mankind have seemed so much more serious. We can no longer do so in a protein-deficient world. For hunger cripples the development of intellect and adequate functioning in a world that requires maximum mental and bodily strength.

Doctors should be doing more for the world in the nature of preventive medicine, and preventive medicine surely takes into consideration a basic diet that is sufficient in proper nutrients.

Consider the conditions of the world's urban areas. Our American slums are horrible enough, but the slums of Calcutta and the barrios of South America are unbelievable. These countries need our help, the help of our doctors, in pushing for medical reforms and food programs for the poor.

Leading nutritionists of our country in testimony before the Senate last year told us that the six months preceding birth and the first six months of life—as well as up to age four—are the greatest periods of brain cell growth. Hence, it is vitally important that pregnant women and girls have adequate protein intake in their diets.

The most shocking thing I have heard nutritionists say is that such lack of protein, primarily among the poor, during the greatest period of brain cell growth results in brain retardation which is not recoverable!

It seems to me incumbent upon doctors, particularly, to spearhead programs of education to make the world's people more aware of proper nutrition. Poverty, rural and slum, means starchy diets, lacking proteins; which means pregnant women, improperly fed; which means ill-fed fetuses in their wombs; which means fetuses which fail to synthesize proteins and brain cells at normal rates; which means a high rate of mortality among babies, and a high rate of mental retardation as well.

When you consider the fact that 75 percent of the mental retardation in this country occurs in poor urban and rural areas, and when you consider the role that malnutrition can play in a child's inability to learn, then I think you can see how serious this problem is. Although these figures concern the United States, they are applicable to the world, two-thirds of whose people live in poverty and hunger.

Our Lord, in his Sermon on the Mount, said:

Blessed are you poor, for yours is the kingdom of God.
Blessed are you that hunger now, for you shall be satisfied.
Blessed are you that weep now, for you shall laugh (Luke 6:20–21, RSV).

And the following words should give us pause:

But woe to you that are rich, for you have received your consolation.
Woe to you that are full now, for you shall hunger.
Woe to you that laugh now, for you shall mourn and weep (Luke 6:20–25, RSV).

Jesus' mission centered among the poor and outcast of his society.

The median family income in this country is eight thousand dollars a year. In some countries of the world it is *not* a hundred dollars a year, but less.

We can do more to redress the grievances of the scarred, angry, and undernourished peoples of our world. That is, if they want our aid; we cannot force it upon them.

But, first, we must stop this multi-million-dollar traffic in arms to countries which cannot feed their people—India, Pakistan, Latin America; the list is long.

We need more programs on a people-to-people basis, such as Food for Peace and the Peace Corps. Surplus grain worth hundreds of millions of dollars has been used to feed starving peoples.

Perhaps we could, if China faces another famine as it has in the past, hold out the hand of friendship to this potential enemy by offering China our food.

Why not? Can you imagine Jesus Christ hating the hungry Chinese *just* because they live under a Communist political system? Did he not say to love our enemies? And is not giving food loving one's enemies?

Consider the Peace Corps. Tens of thousands of American men and women have volunteered two years of service to working with the people of the developing countries. The work of these volunteers has often been downgraded by so-called "realists" who have difficulty in measuring the impact of the corps. Perhaps they are using the wrong criteria. They want to see economic "evidence" of success, where our efforts have been primarily humanitarian. Unfortunately, they are oriented totally toward measuring "progress" in strictly economic terms, and they have difficulty giving proper weight to more elusive signs of progress, such as lowered disease rates, higher literacy, and expanded opportunities for human understanding.

There are other examples of direct aid programs for humanitarian purposes. Project Hope, since its inception at the forefront of the People-to-People programs nearly ten years ago, has operated the S.S. *Hope*. More than 8,450 major operations have been performed aboard this unique ship and some one hundred thousand persons have been treated. Perhaps the greatest accomplishment in this undertaking has been the training of 3,450 local doctors and nurses in the latest medical techniques.

The operational cost of S.S. *Hope* is about five million dollars a year. This is less than the F-14 fighter plane which the Navy will begin to buy in 1970 at a cost of almost eight million dollars each, to be used on a one billion dollar nuclear aircraft carrier, which may be obsolete.

Poverty, disease, pollution, and low standards of living are cyclic. Unless the cycle can be interrupted, success is elusive.

Medicine is a principal tool capable of breaking the cycle, permitting a healthier people an opportunity to raise their living standards, reduce poverty, and use their God-given human potential.

I have discussed a healthy society as a necessary component of a progressive society. I want to relate this medical factor to the biggest question mark of our age—*our ability to survive in an unstable world.*

The delicate balance of survival depends to a great degree on the maintenance of political stability in the emerging nations of the world. But political stability cannot be developed in a sick, malnourished, parasite-infected and apathetic populace.

The Middle East today offers a poignant and sobering example of this truth. From my own travel experiences in Israel and the Arab nations, I have become convinced that at the roots of these hostile tensions are years of deprivation and suffering undergone by those displaced as refugees. The neglected human needs of these unfortunate people—needs for nutrition, housing, and medical care—were part of the breeding grounds for the animosity that exists today and the resultant costly political instability.

To take another example, the late Dr. Tom Dooley, the God-inspired founder of medical hospitals in Laos—and quite primitive hospitals they were—found that those river people, in a land of two million souls, had no medical doctors! Disease was widespread just because of the lack of such an ordinary commodity as soap!

Mark Hatfield

The Laotians had no soap to wash wounds. They didn't even know what soap was for, and wounds were left to fester in the hot climate. Dr. Dooley, his nurses and volunteers, and young Laotian assistants helped change the lives of thousands of wounded people *with soap.*

When Dr. Dooley died of cancer, others picked up the cause. American know-how and the compassion of young American doctors and nurses continue today to do more in that war-torn country than the bombs of Vietnam to save a grieving world.

I believe very firmly that medicine should become a primary part of our foreign aid programs. Human values must be accepted as equal to our economic values, and the field of medicine is virtually untapped. Yet our medical resources, our gifted doctors, nurses, and technicians possess incalculable potential for positive results in human development.

The potential lies in building bodies, treating disease, reducing pollution, controlling population, and strengthening pride and self-respect.

Our State Department must give higher priority to medical programs. Despite the best of intentions, the Agency for International Development has placed a low priority upon health education needs. And technical assistance has not included significant contributions to health needs similar to those provided for communications, road building, hydroelectric plants, and metallurgical and agricultural projects.

We are in competition with Communist ideology for the minds and hearts of the peoples of the world—particularly the underdeveloped nations. As John Kennedy said, "Democracy is the hope of the world. Communism, like totalitarianism, is as old as the pyramids."

We can win the hearts of the peoples of the world if we

bind up their wounds, if we show them how to grow enough food, if we educate their children, and if we love them. We cannot win them by bombing defenseless and hungry women and children. You can help by writing to the president and the State Department encouraging them to include health programs high on the agenda for foreign aid.

I believe, with the religious poet and anthropologist Loren Eiseley, that man is in the process of evolving into a more spiritual being. We have, indeed, been civilized only nine thousand years, and we have much to learn. And part of that learning process is to give of what we have—ourselves, our learning—to those who have not.

This is God's work, and we should all be at it. For there are demonic forces at work in the world which will destroy the world's potential for good unless the forces of righteousness increase their numbers.

Manpower must be found in this country to work on medical problems abroad. This is a touchy area, since many experts consider medical programs in the United States to be understaffed. We need fifty-two thousand doctors and yet the medical schools are turning out only eight thousand a year.

Nevertheless, the medical schools could contribute much to our overseas programs. For instance, students could volunteer to serve as instructors in medical education programs abroad during the summer months. Students from medical schools operating on a quarter system could be used at other than summer periods. Volunteers would be expected to spend three or four months abroad, initiating training programs for middle-level technical assistants in sanitation, laboratory work, x-ray, and population control techniques.

Not only would such a program be a tremendous boon to the training of medical personnel in the developing countries, but it would have many advantages for the medical

Mark Hatfield

student and medical profession in this country. The student would be exposed to a variety of diseases in a variety of environments previously known only from textbooks, thus broadening his perspective. Medical schools could benefit from the overseas contacts and opportunities to improve their reservoirs of teaching materials—slides, photographs, specimens and so forth, brought back by returning students.

Schools of nursing and dietetics could also benefit by enabling volunteer third- or fourth-year students to join the program to offer instruction in the fundamentals of nursing, dietetics, nutrition, and statistics. If our medical schools so desired, they could make substantive contributions in the people-to-people health programs through a modification of their respective curricula to permit participation on a credit-earning basis of student volunteers in various programs.

Supervision of American medical students could be done through the use of volunteer civilian physicians assigned to the Peace Corps or by those working with a volunteer medical care program such as Project Hope, Care-Medico, or Project Concern. Supervision could also be provided by retired medical officers of the services overseas, State Department physicians, or retired civilians.

We could also put more medical ships into service. The S.S. *Hope* could serve as a prototype for a small fleet of hospital ships. They could operate along the lines of the *Hope*'s schedule with a ten-month stay in port where the ship serves as a hospital base and center for medical education ashore. When the ship departs, the education teams could stay behind until the host country has become more self-sufficient.

More than one ship would be required. And as I stated before, the S.S. *Hope* costs about five million dollars a year to operate. But ships could be obtained by the federal government and the operation of them could be turned over to an organization similar to Project Hope. With the decline in ocean travel, the possibility presents itself for the United States to obtain obsolete ocean liners, as well as outmoded naval vessels, refit them as hospital ships, subsidize their operational costs, and offer them to private nonprofit foundations.

To elevate the health of a nation it is first necessary to begin with simplistic forms of medical assistance designed to eliminate common diseases, provide instruction in personal and public hygiene, establish immunization programs, and assist in developing proper waste disposal methods suited to the local environment. Much disease in foreign lands results from the open trench method of sewage disposal in the villages.

Dietetic technicians, statisticians, practical nurses, and birth control specialists will be in equal demand to assist in the education of selected indigenous personnel. The primary purpose will be to acquaint those local personnel with the importance to them and their nation of the need to overcome malnutrition, develop a reliable census and valid vital statistics, provide the essentials of midwifery and contraceptive information, and establish basic health education programs.

The development of middle-level medical training programs is the key to providing basic fundamentals of public health, sanitation, and medical care in rural areas. Bringing promising young men and women to the United States to learn these skills is often self-defeating. In our medical schools they learn techniques which are too sophisticated for the facilities in their own countries.

The only place they can really put their hard-won knowledge to full use is in the United States. This fact, plus the more comfortable living standards they can enjoy in Amer-

Mark Hatfield

ica, contribute to a serious medical "brain drain" from the developing nations.

Dr. Dooley learned to train native Laotians to treat patients and dispense medicines. In fact, he dispensed very little himself; he only treated the sick. He always required payment as well. It need be only something small, in kind, a chicken or an egg, in order to preserve the self-respect of the person treated. This is most important in any overseas work.

I believe that the reorientation of our foreign aid programs toward more humanitarian objectives can be successful; more successful than we dream possible.

Foreign aid has two long-range goals. The first, too long ignored, is the humanitarian effort to feed the hungry, alleviate the suffering of the diseased, and improve the environment of the impoverished. The second goal, long the overriding ambition of our assistance programs, is to encourage economic development.

But what our foreign assistance policy-makers often fail to take into account is the extent to which economic development depends on human development.

Jacob Kaplan, author of *The Challenge of Foreign Aid*, finds evidence that investment in social programs, such as improved education, health, and housing may return higher dividends in terms of the national standard of living than strictly economic investment, for an industrially based society requires a highly educated citizenry. Even more to the point, an energetic, progressive society must be a healthy society.

As a nation we should recognize that our influence and power consists not only of our economic and military strength, but also of our human values and the priorities we give to the well-being of people.

We have been disappointed with multi-billion-dollar foreign aid programs which did not buy friends and allies and only increased the hostility of the poorer nations toward us. Surely it is time to try another, more humanitarian approach. Such humanitarianism does not place too great a burden upon our medical community, if we are truly dedicated to alleviating human suffering abroad.

Ways and means can be found to tap the vast medical resources at home for use abroad if, in fact, a realignment of priorities is accepted in this country. The medical schools can produce enough physicians for this country as well as the work abroad if they will to do so, and if the federal government helps with financial aid.

Medicine has a precise and identifiable role which needs exploitation, development, and direct involvement in the formulation of American foreign policy.

It can be orchestrated into that foreign policy and serve to brighten our image abroad. It can contribute to political stability and economic viability by raising the standards of health in the developing nations.

Within the American people there is a long tradition of voluntaryism and a great reservoir of compassion for the less fortunate peoples of the world. I am sure that, given worthwhile and meaningful programs, there will be no shortage of volunteers to serve the medical needs of humanity. The medical profession, especially, should make a full contribution to these programs. Of all the professions in this country, it is the one most fundamentally committed to the alleviation of suffering, and to the unselfish service of mankind.

Part Two:

A LIFE TO
EXPLORE

Searching and
Being Found

*When one looks back upon his own spiritual
pilgrimage, he often senses that it has
not only been his personal search for God,
but also God's search for him—seeking,
pursuing, and finally grasping him. Although
one's encounter with the Person of Christ is a
process of continual growth and change, there
are often certain pivotal points which become
markers along the path. I wanted to share with
others my own spiritual journey—so I tried to
summarize it by writing the following words a
few years ago. Reading them again and thinking
back over my life, I continue to stand in amaze-
ment at the changes and experiences that
continually intersect my life because of my
encounter with Jesus Christ.*

Searching and Being Found

THERE IS A WORD IN OUR LAN-
guage which we don't hear
very often today, and yet I
believe it plays a part in every successful life. The word is
"commitment."

Commitment to an ideal was a familiar word in our
home. Eventually the idea of commitment became a kind
of standard to me, in every area of my life but one. I came
to share not only my family's abhorrence of corruption in
government, but also their respect and admiration for
those leaders who upheld the most noble precepts of our
nation. My childhood heroes included nearly as many political figures as cowboys and athletes.

I'll never forget the time that James Farley, one of these
heroes, visited Salem, Oregon. Our school band welcomed
him at the capitol where he was to give a speech. After the
program, he shook hands with each member of the band

and thanked us for playing. This greatly impressed us, but we were really thrilled when we later received personal letters of thanks from Washington, D.C. I framed my letter and placed it among my most prized boyhood possessions.

Through the influence of such men and the encouragement of my parents, I began seriously to consider a political career. Through reading, I acquainted myself with great leaders of the past and the present and tried to discover the secrets of their success. I discovered that the most effective leaders were those who dedicated themselves to the highest ideals and who worked unceasingly for the realization of them. From the enthusiasm of Jefferson to the dedication of Lincoln there was a contagious spirit about them, and I found myself dreaming of how best to serve my country.

This boyhood dream developed later into an earnest desire to become a politician, and all my education was directed to that end. I became more practical as the years passed and began adopting certain rules for political success.

In politics, for example, it was easy for me to see the value of commitment. In fact, I used to expound it to my classes when I was a political science teacher at Willamette University in Salem, Oregon.

"Take a stand!". . ."Join a party, meet the candidates, ring doorbells, get involved.". . ."Get down off the bleachers and into the rough-and-tumble where the issues of life are decided."

In 1950, to prove my point further, I announced that I was going to file my name as a candidate for the state legislature. My students thought this was a great idea. On the day that I walked across the campus to the state capitol to put my hat into the ring, a band with more members than harmony marched along behind me playing "The Battle Hymn of the Republic." Maybe it was the band—

later they accompanied me on speaking tours—but we ended by winning the election.

After winning the election and serving two terms in the lower house, I went on to the state senate. In the meantime, I was appointed dean of students at the university. All of these honors were highly encouraging to me as an aspiring young politician. But with these outward advancements came a disturbing inner awareness of inadequacy in the area of my spiritual life. It was during this time that I first began to face that part of my life where there was no commitment: religion.

One of my major duties as dean of students was to counsel college men who sought advice regarding academic or personal problems. The tremendous responsibility of this task was overwhelming. I often felt that the spiritual problems they presented were not completely answered in my own life and that I had no right to counsel others on matters which I had not worked out personally. This fact affected not only my position as dean of students but also my entire career. If I could offer little real spiritual help to individuals, what did I have to offer the state or the nation or the world?

Not only did I wonder about my personal spiritual inadequacies, but I also began to think about my purpose in life and my motive for living. This resulted primarily from my contact with a group of students who had asked me to serve as adviser to a Bible study group. These students, many of whom became my very close friends, by their lives and by the goals for which they were striving brought to mind some of the things I had heard in church about what Jesus Christ wanted of us.

I'd gone to church, literally, all my life. Having grown up in a home where church and the Bible were a way of life, I guess I picked up the external attitudes that go with genuine religious life. During World War II, I was assigned to

Mark Hatfield

landing-craft ferrying troops ashore on Okinawa and Iwo Jima. In those invasions there weren't enough chaplains to bury the dead, let alone listen to the fears and hopes of the living. Temporary additional chaplains were assigned from among the men. In our unit I was given the job.

So, obviously, since other people believed I had a real religion, I believed it myself. Religion came very naturally to me. That was just the trouble; it was too automatic. It was a religion of habit, not of commitment.

It took me a long time to discover the difference. But I remember vividly the night in 1954 when it all came to a head. I was sitting alone in my room in my parents' home. For months my words in the classroom had been coming back to mock me. I was urging my students to stand up and be counted, but I was a very silent and very comfortable Christian. That night in the quiet of my room the choice was suddenly made clear. I could not continue to drift along as I had been doing, going to church because I had always gone, because everyone else went, because there wasn't any particular reason not to go. Either Christ was God and Savior and Lord or he wasn't; and if he were, then he had to have all my time, all my devotion, all my life.

I made the choice that night, many years ago; I *committed* myself to Christ. I saw that for thirty-one years I had lived for self, and I decided I wanted to live the rest of my life for Jesus Christ. I asked God to forgive my self-centeredness and to make me his own. I was assured by the words of Paul, "Therefore if any man be in Christ, he is a new creature: old things are passed away; behold, all things are become new" (2 Cor. 5:17).

Following Jesus Christ has been an experience of increasing challenge, adventure, and happiness. How true are his words: "I am come that they might have life, and that they might have it more abundantly" (John 10:10). It is not to a life of ease and mediocrity that Christ calls us, but to the disciple-like, Christ-empowered life. No matter what field we are in, we are called to give our complete allegiance to him. No cause, noble as it may seem, can be satisfying or purposeful without the direction of Christ. I can say with all sincerity that living a committed Christian life is truly satisfying because it has given me true purpose and direction by serving not myself, but Jesus Christ.

Now, the decisions, the policies, and the programs which I follow in my official life I try to root first of all in prayer. I believe that the Lord is interested in leading in this important job, and I depend upon him for counsel. This does not mean that every decision I make is the right one, that every policy which I have is the correct one; but I feel that these matters are of such importance that I do commit them to the Lord. When they are wrong, they are errors in my judgment and not his, and they are perhaps examples of where I tried to get ahead of God's leading.

It seems obvious that man is not isolated from outside forces which have direct bearing upon his present and his future. Whether he wants to tread life's road alone, groping for his own objectives, or whether he wishes to have an understanding of life and the future it holds for him, it is his choice to make. One can only learn about life as one learns about God. A relationship with God, as revealed in Jesus Christ, is the highest relationship which man can achieve.

Mark Hatfield

A Living Dialogue

Several years ago I first wrote about the meaning of my own dialogue with God through the Scriptures. Today the Word of God continues to have an enriching relevance for my life, revealing new insights and fresh truths that stimulate my inward growth as a follower of Christ.

A Living Dialogue

GOD IS NOT A MYSTERIOUS Being who has isolated himself completely from us. He has taken the initiative to communicate with us in a way we can understand. He has given us the Bible, which is so readily available to us for reading, studying, exploring, discussing, and teaching. In the Bible we learn who God is and what he desires of man. Christ established the pattern for our relation with God, with our neighbors, and with society. He makes his own power available to us for a more abundant life.

I do not regard the Bible as a bedtime story to prepare me for a restful night. Nor is it simply an order of worship to be used on Sunday mornings. Since it is the source of God's truth, we need to be saturated with it. We need to delve into it systematically, with enthusiasm, with curiosity, and with willingness to apply God's will as it unfolds to us. Often I need the peace and refreshment of the Book of Psalms. On other occasions, I need the assurance of God's unfailing, unchanging, eternal, and personal love for me as it is wonderfully revealed in the New Testament.

It is through the message of the Bible that we meet Jesus Christ and become committed to him. Then naturally and increasingly our selfish motives and actions are revealed to us. We seek God's forgiveness and move to a higher plane of living. This constant interaction with God, through the Scriptures, is the only way to maintain a healthy Christian life.

Part Three:

THE QUALITY OF
OUR LEADERSHIP

The Atypical Man

John Gardner's writings, as well as others, have impressed upon me the crisis of leadership that exists in our society and the cult of conformity that entraps so many and subdues their true potential. From a Christian perspective, the need is even more urgent for those who will act with a singularity of purpose and a resolution of will—those who will not mouth the superficial slogans nor be engulfed by the comfortable conventions of a religious subculture. When Sören Kierkegaard wrote "Purity of the Heart Is to Will One Thing," he was touching on the quality of leadership that infects the lives of those individual men who make a difference. Christendom, as well as our nation, stands in desperate need of men who are called forth with clear and unswerving sense of purpose. That is the way allegiance to Christ can and should transform one's life, as I tried to point out in this 1969 speech.

The Atypical Man

WHEN WE THINK OF ANY event in our history which is accepted as being "significant," we are usually reminded of an individual or a small handful of men—men who made the difference in that situation.

Eric Hoffer has said that "the game of history is usually played by the best and the worst over the heads of the majority in the middle." Paul Tournier alluded to a similar notion by suggesting that less than 7 percent of the people have independent minds. Who will make up that relatively small group of pacesetters in each of our communities? in each of the states? in each of the nations of the world? What kind of man will it take to make the difference? Who will provide the leadership as the complexities of society develop in proportions almost beyond human comprehension?

From my perspective there has never been a greater

demand for positive, creative, committed leadership—at every level, in every area—than today. We need a leadership that dominates change rather than one that merely reacts to it. We need a leadership with broad knowledge, great vision, and a commitment to serving the needs of others rather than one that feeds on opportunities for personal gain.

Whatever trust we put in our technology, whatever faith we put in our system of government, our future depends on the quality of leadership we can develop. I would like to describe the characteristics of that man who I think can and will make the difference whenever the situation calls for excellence in leadership.

But first let me share some things which I feel hinder the development of the kind of leaders we need in greater abundance today and will need in the years ahead. The fact that these phenomena exist is bad enough, but the trends are even more disturbing.

In our mass society, we are driven to view life in terms of averages, categories, and the "typical" man. We are appealed to by mass media, by form letters. We are known not by our names and personalities, but we are known to faceless computers by a network of numbers assigned to us. We can all sympathize with the student who carried a placard reading "I am a human being—do not fold, bend, spindle, or mutilate." We reward conformity while we frown on initiative and creativity. We disregard quality for quantity, individual satisfaction for volume, and personal attention for mass production. Thus, mediocrity becomes our accepted standard and the average becomes the ideal. The result of all this is the production of "leaders" who are no more than followers, who look first to see where the crowd is going, then scramble to get to the head of the line.

A cause and a symptom of the loss of individuality is our increasing dependence on our institutions. We demand "efficiency," and in our quest for an economy of effort, we consolidate our smaller groups into larger organizations.

No one person is able to comprehend the size or the complexity of the many institutions with which he must deal. And since he cannot understand them, he resigns himself to accept them for whatever they are. He loses his will to alter them for the better. He becomes complacent. Since a man's well-being often depends on how he is treated by the institution for which he works, he soon learns not to rock the boat. Within the complexity of the organization, no one person can be an expert in everything; thus specialists are bred. No one is willing to accept the responsibility for the activity or the coordination of the institution. It is too easy to pass the buck endlessly from one specialist to the next.

For the man caught in the institutional web, internal or spiritual values are hard to discern. Materialism becomes the order of the day, and the dollar is king. A man's worth is measured by what he *has*, not by what he *is*. While the inner man remains void, the external man is constantly indulged. People place their faith in things and believe naïvely that money can solve any problem. A man looks at his fellow-men and thinks of status rather than of service. So long as he can postpone the confrontation with his inner emptiness, he will keep himself preoccupied with the external world, remaining comfortably deluded about the quality of his life. His affluence affords him countless means of escape from the hard reality of his own shallowness.

This is by no means a complete picture. Other phenomena are at work in modern society which stifle individual expression and blunt man's potential for dynamic leadership. It is sad to think that these conditions exist even in the best of homes, in the best of schools, and, yes, in the best of churches.

Mark Hatfield

So what do we do?

Rousseau looked upon complacency with despair when he said, "As soon as any man says of the affairs of State 'what does it matter' the State may be given up for lost."

John Gardner was slightly more optimistic when he said, "It is hard for Americans to realize that the survival of the idea for which this nation stands is not inevitable. It may survive if enough Americans care enough. . . . It would be easier for us to grasp this truth if we weren't so blessedly comfortable. Part of our problem is how to stay awake on a full stomach. And the fateful question remains open: Can we as a people, despite the narcotic of easy living and the endless distractions of a 'well-heeled' society, respond with vigor and courage and dedication to the demands that history has placed upon us?"

The answer to the complexities of mass society lies with the individual, who has almost, but not quite, vanished. Our temptation is to try to solve our problems through bigger and better organizations, by raising more money, by passing more laws. But, as Daniel Webster said, "The things that are wrong with the country are the sum total of all the things that are wrong with us as individuals." And centuries before our country was founded, Socrates advised, "Let him that would move the world, first move himself."

I cannot answer these questions for others, but I know the answer I have found. If an individual is willing to put the person of Jesus Christ first in his life, I believe he has the greatest chance of being a leader who can make a difference. The leader who is committed to Christ is uniquely prepared and equipped to take his place in American society and make his influence felt there.

The leader committed to Christ is a man of purpose. He need not guess, wonder, or speculate about the nature of man and the nature of the universe. He knows where he came from and where he will ultimately go. He is committed, not to a cause or an ideal, but to a Person. He knows whom he serves, and he knows also that he cannot serve two masters. He does not feel the frustration of being compelled to please everyone. He believes that his existence and the existence of the universe have reason and purpose, though he sometimes cannot discern just what that purpose is. In his small way he can participate in and affirm that divine purpose, and with such a vision he pursues excellence in all things.

The leader who is committed to Christ is a man of power. Though he is well aware of his own weaknesses, he is not bound by his own limitations, for he can do all things through Christ who strengthens him. Power and authority do not frighten him, though he respects them; he knows his life is bound up in the One who has ultimate authority and ultimate power. With such a relationship to give him security, he can act out of confidence, "For God did not give us a spirit of timidity but a spirit of power and love and self-control" (1 Tim. 1:7, RSV). As he encounters temptation, he recognizes it for what it is and knows he has God's word that no temptation can come to him unless a means of endurance or escape has also been provided.

The Christian leader is a man of perspective. He is a whole man, a complete man. His education, environment, and physical well-being all take their proper place in his life; none is put out of proportion. The material world retains the importance it deserves, for it is a trust of which man is steward. Yet material things are seen as means to serve God through their proper use, rather than ends in themselves. The Christian does not feel driven by an unquenchable and idolatrous thirst for money, for he knows the One who ultimately owns everything. As so many American young people discover the falseness in materialism, they rightly reject its hollow values. Yet it is tragic to see them abandoning one value system only to find themselves at a loss for something to put in its place. Here Christian leaders can fill the gap by demonstrating Christ's blend of the material and the spiritual.

The leader who is dedicated to Christ is a man of peace, for he serves a God of love. He does not try to make peace out of his own strength or the goodness of his own heart. Rather, because he seeks to "love God with all his heart, soul, mind, and strength" he is better able to "love his neighbor as himself." He sees every man, without prejudice or favoritism, as a creation of God, redeemed or potentially redeemed by Christ. Thus, even though he may disagree with another person's ideas, he can accept and respect the other person on the basis of their shared origin. At peace with his Creator and with himself, the Christian can become a true peacemaker among other men, for he will radiate the attitude of peace in all his relationships.

The man committed to Christ is a servant, though he may also be a leader. Following the example of Jesus, he serves for the sake of service, not for the rewards it may bring his way. He cannot isolate himself from the needs of the world, and when he encounters those needs, he is compelled to try to fill them. For him, complacency is not a live option. He knows he should be no less concerned for man's total well-being than was Christ, who instructed that "whoever would be great among you must be your servant, and whoever would be first among you must be slave of all" (Mark 10:43–44, RSV).

These are the reasons that a man committed to Jesus Christ makes a difference. He recognizes his purpose in living; he has resources and strength from beyond himself; he puts the things of the world in proper perspective; he knows the worth of the individual and of relationships among men; and he truly wishes to be a servant.

Conflict and Conscience   **114**

This is the quality of life which Christ offers us. It amazes me that more people have not accepted the challenge of the Christian adventure. The man of Christ is not merely a man of theological contemplation; he is a man of action. If you and I are willing to take Christ at his word, our action in the world will have far-reaching effects, and we will be men who make a difference.

Mark Hatfield

Authority vs. Love?

The impact of Young Life, a nondenominational Christian group which works with high-school students across the country, has always won my highest respect. Their innovative and provocative journal, Focus on Youth, *always seems to bring new and lively perspectives on the young people of our time and the relevance of the Good News to their lives. The editors of* Focus on Youth *told me they were preparing an issue devoted to the question of authority and asked me to contribute some thoughts. It was a challenge, for it is difficult to know how genuine and respected authority can replace the haughty authoritarianism that destroys so many relationships and deepens the polarization in our land. I tried to give briefly my perspective and views of this troubling dilemma in the chapter which follows.*

Authority vs. Love?

AMERICA IS IN A DARK MOOD. It searches its national soul as it faces a crisis of revolutionary proportions. Whether this crisis will be resolved by means of a peaceful evolutionary process of change or through violent revolution hinges on the reaction of mature Americans.

You and I together can create a framework for reconciliation, or we can further divide and polarize the extremes of our society. I have faith that America can renew its foundations. No one man, however, can create the right conditions. No one commission in Washington can heal the division in this nation. Our problems are fundamentally an expression of our whole social, political, and economic environment. Essentially we have failed in our understanding of man. We have not discovered how to live with ourselves. The answer for America must lie in our ability to react responsibly to the authority invested in us wherever we are—as parents, as teachers, as workers, or as political figures.

In all candor, we must begin by looking at ourselves and our own families. Authority, after all, begins in the home. The decline of respect for law and authority has at least part of its roots in our homes. It is in our homes that we discover how authority, if it is to be accepted, must be set forth in the framework of love. And with our children we learn that authentic love and concern for them must include firm authority.

Authority without love becomes authoritarianism, the futile attempt to rule by brute force. Love that ignores authority becomes mere sentimentality, the naïve belief that responsibility is the result of permissiveness.

To exercise authority in the framework of love is the task for us all, whether it be in our individual families or in our nation. We know that there will be no peace and no harmony among us if we believe that authority precludes love or that love denies authority.

We could identify our national crises as the Vietnam War, poverty, alienated youth, or the disadvantaged minorities; but I believe a deeper malaise infects our country —a decline of respect for authority. There is really nothing new about this trend. Man has always felt a tension between his civilization as it is and as he wishes it to be. Man is never wholly "at ease in Zion." We should not then be greatly surprised by the tensions which rip and strain at our traditions.

In evaluating our American scene we must be mindful that we are not only born and bred in revolution but that we touched the brink of disaster in our Civil War barely a century ago. Only the most idealistic utopian could have failed to foresee many of our present-day tensions. They are as old (and as young) as our country. Violence, lawlessness, draft resistance, police strikes, and civil disorders can claim ample precedent in our past.

Behind many of these issues are larger questions of conscience. They present themselves to thoughtful persons in every age and are never easily or wholly resolved. They include the nature and rightful use of the state and its authority, the responsiveness of society to pressures for change, the relation between order and dissent, the needful redress of rightful grievance, and the difficulty of civil disobedience.

The distinction between power and authority is confusing to most of us. Proper authority is not rooted in force. It is built into the very fabric of human association through respect or loyalty. To win and to deserve allegiance, authority must be both responsible and responsive. There must be a sense of limitation and restraint in its exercise. Its operations must embody justice and equity. Above all, a free society must provide legitimate ways for its citizens to seek "redress of grievances." This precaution becomes necessary as we recognize the inescapable fact that a human community is always faulty. But by no means does it suggest that we should throw up our hands and give up trying to improve. It does mean that we share the obligation to provide lawful channels for dissent. When such channels are absent or defective, frustration and resentment give rise to rebellion and violence. Naked power rises to take the place of authority.

We also have to establish a clear distinction between protest and subversion. Protest and redress, in the proper context, are acts of faith in the democratic process, not traitorous moves to be clubbed and curtailed into submission. The task of making politics relevant to society's genuine needs is one of making the power structure responsive

Mark Hatfield

to the voices of its citizenry. Authority is not a defense of the status quo. It does in fact assure the right to change, where that change will benefit the majority.

Wherever authority is interpreted in terms of coercion, we have authoritarianism, which destroys integrity. Authority in the best sense nurtures understanding; both authoritarianism and anarchy subvert understanding and lead to the exercise of raw power—the naked conflict of will with will. This trust is affirmed supremely in the Bible where God's power is always associated with his authority, which is grounded in justice and in love.

The responsibility of all who would restore the foundations in a time of trouble is to work for understanding rather than for brute forms of coercion. To humanize the establishment, to create and maintain channels of communication between groups in conflict, to discern the signs of the times and to act in the light of that discernment for the well-being of the body politic—these are tasks which are ours today and tomorrow.

Students question America. They question the reasons for adhering to our democratic process. Their doubts arise because they know of our many failures. I believe that young people feel alienated from our political process not because they fail to believe in democracy, but because they do believe and have seen it fail to function adequately in meeting what they consider to be their needs.

It is my firm conviction that with the passionate involvement of committed youth, our structures can be disturbed, shaken, and then renewed. They must be revitalized, however, to enhance human freedom, to encourage social responsibility, and to establish greater relevance between people and their institutions. The real crisis lies in our human relationships—the deterioration of authority, of trust, of concern and dignity and hope.

The '70s can be marked by creative perspectives and a

whole new understanding of our nation's priorities. These will result in significant progress toward full justice, restored sanity, and even lasting peace—at home and throughout the world.

Thinking young men and women who are willing to act sensibly for what they believe can direct our technology toward the service of human need. They can replace coercive power with meaningful involvement. They can control military force by moral strength. They can give themselves to worthy purposes and find meaning for their lives. But the achievement of these goals will require the all-out commitment of reconciled persons.

The prayer of Jesus which ascribes "the kingdom, the power, and the glory" to God is a chastening rebuke to human authority which is often proud and pretentious—a reminder that power must be tempered with humility, that it must be subject to an ultimate authority—the authority of God.

Mark Hatfield

The Challenge
of Excellence

*Christians who excuse their own mediocrity
with pious rationalizations seem guilty of not
understanding the extent of God's call on their
lives. This conviction, gathered from experience
during my years of service as a university professor and dean of students, motivated me to
write these words about five years ago.*

The Challenge of Excellence

AT THIS TIME IN HISTORY WE have the greatest opportunity and the gravest responsibility to a total commitment to Jesus Christ. We must make an impact upon our associates, our institutions, and our society.

Each of us has a program to execute. Let us do it in such superb manner that people will never equate mediocrity with the things of Christ. Instead let them say that these men and women who meet in Bible-study groups, in prayer, and in fellowship groups are people of worth—people to be relied upon.

Does your work show a marked degree of excellence? Are you committed to the proposition that Christian work should represent a quality or standard of performance that is superior to anything secular, that you are never to be satisfied with mediocrity?

A great god is abroad in our land today—the god of mediocrity, the god of the average. During my days on a college campus, I frequently would hear a student say, "Well, when you come right down to it, I can be happy with a C." Invariably, my response was, "You have the capacity to do A work and you are doing C work. I have less respect for you than for the one who does C work because that is the extent of his capacity."

Occasionally, the student would excuse himself by saying he was so busy in a Christian campus organization and just too involved for the Lord and would have to settle for a C that semester. To such a person I'd say his first responsibility was to utilize and mobilize all the resources, capacity, intellect, drive, and ambitions that God has given him and to use them to the fullest. In dedication to Christ, a commitment to your endeavor is primary.

If you are in an educational institution, that is your first responsibility—to perform to the highest degree of your intellectual ability. That excellent performance will become a witness to the Lord you serve. If it means you go out one night less to an extracurricular activity, it is better to do that and to have people see that a Christian is a person of excellence, ability, and high standards.

No words, no speech-making, no meetings or sessions—though they be religious—can substitute in the thinking of the unbeliever for a performance of mediocrity. He judges that you are merely using that as a crutch or an alibi rather than doing that to which you are educationally committed.

Each of us has a program to execute. Let us do it in such superb manner that people will never equate mediocrity with the things of Christ.

From Curiosity
to Commitment

During the past years, I have been fortunate enough to address the governors' prayer breakfasts held in various states. These are annual gatherings of civic, business, government, and community leaders who come to reflect upon the relevance of spiritual values in their vocational tasks and their personal lives. When I was asked to address the California governor's prayer breakfast in early 1970, I thought again about the challenge of speaking to an essentially unchurched group of people who were meeting for some kind of a religious purpose. It seems to me that many people have nothing to do with Christian commitment because they reject the religious institutions, with all their so-called hypocrisy and failures, in our society. At the same time, I have sensed an authentic and growing curiosity about transcendent or spiritual matters that is evidenced in many ways today outside of the formal religious establishment. So that morning, I attempted to say that spiritual values can be alive even though religious institutions appear dead.

From Curiosity
to Commitment

I REMEMBER READING *Time* magazine's cover story of April 8, 1966, "Is God Dead?" *Time*'s recent issue at the close of the decade of the '60s on December 26, 1969, featured the cover story, "Is God Coming Back to Life?" It is significant that at the end of a decade marked by alienation, cynicism, and violence, *Time* raises the question of whether God is coming back to life—and that this issue appears during the Christmas season. But perhaps the real question is, "Are people coming alive to God?" It is my conviction that our nation stands in need of a complete spiritual renaissance; our destiny in the coming decade is likely to depend on this factor more than any other.

It is interesting to note the recent decline of our religious institutions. In 1958, 49 percent of the population attended church; ten years later church attendance had dropped to 43 percent. A Gallup Poll recently asserted that a majority of people believed that "religion was losing its influence." I have read estimates that at least four thousand priests left the Catholic church last year. Basically, for all denominations, birth rates are running much higher than baptism rates. It is clear that the religious "establishment" or religious institutions are declining in their vitality and relevance, but this does *not* mean that interest in "spiritual" matters is decreasing. Actually, in most cases that interest and curiosity is simply not being met in our archaic religious institutions.

The contemporary growth of transcendental or spiritual curiosity that can be observed outside of our traditional religious institutions is absolutely fascinating. In my judgment, a cultural revolution is sweeping our society. Television, technical progress, affluence, and increased educational opportunities are all having effects on our culture, and particularly on our young, that we are only beginning to understand. Note the concerns of our youth: they are dissatisfied with materialism, both as a philosophy and a way of life, and are searching for new values and a new life style. In quest of a deeper reality, they are seeking "person-to-person experiences."

Throughout contemporary society I believe there is evidence of a growing interest in forms of spiritual reality. Look at popular fads such as yoga, astrology, and the practice of consulting gurus. Everyone today seems to know his horoscope sign. Recently I read that Parker Brothers says "Ouija Boards" are outselling "Monopoly" as the number one game. Or, consider the growing phenomenon of drug use. People seem to form nearly fanatic religious cults around various patterns of drug use. All of this illustrates a search for a deeper, inner reality—a search which often leads, however, to tragic results. Even popular music and art today express the idea that the external society is superficial and phony, that there is a deeper reality.

We can also turn to the academic field for evidence of this growing curiosity about the spiritual life. Book sales have increased in the areas of religion, metaphysics, transcendental philosophy, and Eastern religions. Recent new scientific journals include the *Journal of Transpersonal Psychology* and a *Journal for the Study of Consciousness*. A program at Duke University has been functioning and gaining academic acceptance for the study of extrasensory perception (ESP). In short, there may be a whole new branch of science and psychology developing—"the science of subjective experience."

Then, notice the contemporary psychological trends and movements. Group therapy, sensitivity training, encounter groups (or "T-groups"), Esalen Institutes, depth psychology, and psychodrama—all are attempts to find "person-changing experiences," ways of discovering the inner self and changing attitudes, values, and behavior.

Finally, look at some of the new religious sects, movements, and cults. They can be found all over the country, but they have grown especially strong in California. Take, for example, the Universal Church of the Master. Half of its members are in California, and they believe in communication with the dead, ESP, etc. Another group is the Self-Realization Fellowship. It is Eastern, Oriental in its background and similar to many different Buddhist sects and cults growing in the United States. Scientology is another example. This cult is devoted to a quest for perfection of the individual and of civilization. It has grown very rapidly in past years with hundreds of thousands of members.

In summary, then, I contend that religious curiosity is very much alive today. It expresses itself in new, strange,

Mark Hatfield

and bizarre ways. But fundamentally, people are seeking spiritual answers to questions about reality, meaning, and purpose in their lives.

Yet, despite this intriguing evidence of the transcendental curiosity that has been developing throughout our society, the signs would hardly indicate that a social paradise is just around the corner. The dominant values that still seem to maintain their hold over our culture are those of materialism. We still find ourselves valuing things more than other people. What we hold in our hands is far more precious to us than what we store up within our hearts. Our shallow commercialism enshrines the ego and makes the selfish concern for our own personal glamour and status the primary goal for millions of us in this society.

The price we pay is the erosion of human relationships among our people. Like a plague hanging over us, the deterioration of trust and human relatedness is more foreboding for our future than any of the commonly cited political problems. Whether it be between man and wife, parent and child, black and white, rich and poor, reactionary and radical, we no longer seem to care even about trying to listen, to communicate, to understand, to trust, and to reconcile.

The divorce rate nationally is now approximately one out of every three or four marriages. In California, nearly one out of every two marriages currently ends in divorce. While it may be difficult to live with others, many find it even harder to live with themselves. Suicides in the United States each year far outnumber the murders.

So, ours is a crisis of values and human relationships. I believe that the final answer to this profound issue can be found in the spiritual dimension in life. That is why I am so intrigued by the growing transcendent curiosity evident today.

But to save ourselves, we must move from curiosity to

Conflict and Conscience

commitment. We must take a "leap of faith" to discover the fullness of life when it is in harmony with God and one's fellow-man.

Now, I do not advocate that we accommodate the message of the faith to the temporary "whims" of society. The problem is not one of making Christianity "relevant," but of discovering its "unchanging relevance." Our faith must be communicated in ways that will be responsive to the present spiritual curiosity; this may certainly mean changing our forms, structures, and methods of expressing our message. But the essential truth of that message does not change.

The spiritual curiosity in society today is a search for more than humanitarian social first-aid given under the guise of religion. The core of Christ's message is what confronts us: God's love can infect people and change their lives; our need is for revitalized, reborn, renewed, committed people with changed values and new attitudes. The direction and purpose of our lives is to be centered in the person of Christ. Such a relation to God results in love of all men, for the source of undying love and compassion for others comes from beyond us. That "God so loved the world" means, as David Poling says, "Not that God loves the roll of church members, and especially those graduated from church-related colleges; not that God loves and prefers the practices of the saints; not that God loves those who help themselves; not that God loves the English-speaking world best and America first; but that God loves the world." [1]

So, our task then is to disperse into the world. "So send I you" were the words of Christ. We must develop a strategy of infiltration which will relate us to the various groups and subcultures in society. Personal involvement is an absolute necessity in meeting the needs of people. We have to identify with and minister to suffering, pain, and alienation

Mark Hatfield

wherever it is found. The demonstration of compassion is the proclamation of one's convictions; we speak not only by what we say, but by what we do. This is what the story of the Good Samaritan tells us. Our mission is to be dispersed into society, living forth God's message of compassion and reconciliation.

Lives That Teach

With four young children in our family, I have come to have great admiration, but little envy, for those who volunteer to be Sunday school teachers. Even though I had some experience in teaching an adult Sunday school class, I still had little idea about what to say to a Sunday school convention I was asked to address. The more I thought about it and talked to friends, the more I became convinced that many of the Christian education programs in our churches today are hopelessly outmoded, blindly propelled by the momentum of tradition. So I decided to come up with specific examples and practical concepts for improving the quality of Christian education in our churches. I do not claim to have any expertise in this field, but I did try to offer some thoughts that might be helpful to those searching for new directions.

Lives That Teach

WE ARE WITNESSING A MASsive failure of Christian education in some of our major denominations. The Sunday school, which originated as a tool to train Christians, has often become just another program that we feel obligated to support. We tend to measure its success by its size rather than by its ability to produce disciples for Christ.

The past failures of Christian education are glaring enough. The really discouraging thing is its present failure in many local churches. We appear to have forgotten that the message of Christ is addressed to the problems of any age. Today we hear so-called Christians decrying campus unrest—but with no concern for the restless. These people are convinced that today's youth are "going to hell fast." But that does not disturb them—they only wish the youth would go more quietly.

We rationalize our attitudes about race without acknowledging our responsibilities. Because we feel we are not directly responsible for the cause of racial problems, we assume that we are not responsible for the solution. On the international level, if a nation threatens the United States, those who claim to be followers of Christ are more likely to call for annihilation than for evangelization. We are able to justify this attitude because we think of another nation in terms of an ideological mass rather than as individuals for whom Christ also died.

It would appear that too much Christian education is aimed at preparing people to live isolated lives in the church, whereas Christ prepared his disciples to live in the world. This may explain why, at a campus protest rally, one young man carried a sign that said "Jesus Yes, Christianity No."

Never has there been a greater need for renewal and redirection in Christian education. It is my desire to discuss six specifics and share my views as a layman and father. I hope that recognizing and meeting some of these "six needs" will help us fulfill our important roles in our Sunday school tasks.

The first need is *recommitment to the primacy of the individual and his relationship to Christ.* While so many persons cry out for individual attention, we offer them committees, boards, membership drives, and stewardship campaigns. Amid all our talk of group awareness, group discussions, group activities, and the role of the church as a functioning unit, it is easy to forget individual needs and the individual's potential lostness and loneliness even among a crowd with shared ideals. Church leadership often remains preoccupied with the details of organization of groups and with providing sufficient building area for group meetings, while particular attention to persons is neglected. If among the structures and sanctuary space of ecclesiastical organization the individual fades from view, then his church has failed him. Nicodemus thought he was getting everything his religion had to offer, and so did many other religious leaders of his day, until the personal attention and concentration of Christ showed them God's particular and individualized love.

In addition, we need to work for an *understanding of the "new openness" in society.* We watch in disapproval and confusion as traditional restraints on behavior and on verbal expression are stripped away. We feel threatened as we sense the shaking of traditional foundations. Our basic assumptions are being questioned, probed, explored, and doubted. In the Sunday school classroom, many questions are being raised which touch the bases of our faith. Yet if our lives are firmly rooted in Christian beliefs, we can listen to and discuss any queries that arise, knowing that the deepest doubts about Christ cannot negate him and human denial cannot nullify him. The Christian can take advantage of society's "new openness" to introduce new honesty into relationships and new avenues into the Christian witness.

Along with an emphasis on the individual and on honesty between individuals goes the need for a *more creative approach in the methods of Christian education.* Flexibility and malleability are the key. Educational methods must respond to the honestly expressed needs of individuals within the learning group. A good look at much of the Sunday school material currently in use in our churches will show that we are far too hung-up on following manuals, quarterlies, and lesson plans written years ago and addressed to the "average" seventh-grader of that time. (And we ask why today's students think the Sunday school experience is irrelevant!) Even the time and place of meeting should not be placed under the restriction of custom. Nothing requires that Sunday school be held in a crowded church basement room at 9:30 Sunday morning—this may be the most distracting and least inspiring setting imaginable. The composition of groups should be subject to innovation, without losing the vital corporate feeling which can be generated in a group that meets together regularly. Joint sessions with groups from other congregations, the meeting together of several families, occasional gatherings of the entire congregation—these and many other new approaches merit experimentation.

Naturally, innovations in group study will require *better preparation on the part of group leaders*—not preparation in the sense of rehearsal, for this would kill the spontaneity of the new situation, but rather a stronger basis in the issues and material to be studied. Sunday school teachers rarely have any professional instruction in the use of reference materials, in the best methods of communicating ideas, or in the ways and means of group leadership. We are in the age of instant communications. Physical difficulties in transmitting ideas have largely been overcome, and what remains is the psychological barrier of the individual's rejection of the message. We are surrounded and bombarded by information, advertisements, and verbiage; messages are cheap; we feel we can afford to pick and choose from others' pleas for attention. People will judge the content of the teacher's message by how well, how persuasively, how attractively it is prepared and presented. Since the church holds in trust the most important message of history, it is worth time and expense to create bold, new programs to upgrade Sunday school teacher training. Remember Paul's words to Timothy: "Do your best to present yourself to God as one approved, a workman who has no need to be ashamed, rightly handling the word of truth" (2 Tim. 2:15, RSV).

New teaching methods will require *new teaching materials*. While our secular schools are being filled with all sorts of new technological equipment, the church sticks to flannelgraphs with pictures of arks. Perhaps some new teaching aids used in our schools can be adapted to Sunday school use. However, we must bear in mind the danger of imagining that flashy teaching materials will take the place of the love and example of a good teacher.

Sunday school training must be just that—training for what will come afterward, for the *daily translation into practical life of our theology*. It is a major tenet of general education that one learns best by doing. Often the doing is necessary to generate motivation for additional study— which should lead in turn to further action. Christian character does not come automatically; it is built by a learning process. Faith, like muscle, grows stronger and more supple with exercise. Our problem is not the lack of knowing; it is the lack of doing. Most Christians *know* far more than they *do*. The authenticity of our Christian faith is tested in everyday life. Christianity is not a spectator sport. The world is keeping track of our behavior; the world hears many profound words but experiences little love and concern. Our witness is dependent much more on the quality and consistency of our living example than on the sentiments we speak. We have set up an artificial barrier between "the message of salvation" and "the works of concern"—a barrier Christ never knew. The love of God cannot be demonstrated in the abstract; it must be shown in real situations as the needs of real persons are met. We need good teachers who can help in the process of translating ideas into action.

The message of Christ comes through people, and it is important what sort of *personal example* they demonstrate to their students. The fruits of the work of Sunday school teachers should be new individuals equipped to do the work of Christ. In one sense the teacher should be reproducing himself, as Paul instructed his pupil Timothy, "what you have heard from me before many witnesses entrust to faithful men who will be able to teach others also" (2 Tim. 2:2, RSV). But, as Paul also says, the teacher must be imitated, yet only as he imitates Christ. Setting a good example requires dependency on, and inspiration by, the Holy Spirit. Without such a life that radiates Christ and reproduces itself through example, the Sunday school teacher will undoubtedly consider his task frustrating, pointless, time-consuming, unrewarding, and fruitless.

As our various churches work to implement these new ideas, we will need *unity among those directing and teaching* in the local congregations. Though individual attention is needed, individuality must be subordinated to the good of the church when it threatens to injure relationships. Consider the powerful influence of ten or fifteen Sunday school teachers who display the teachings of Christ in their relationships with each other. Through sheer example, they could instill a new spirit which, in time, could turn the congregation and the local community upside down—or, as is more often necessary, right side up.

The words of our Lord must be applied with particular intensity, "By this all men will know that you are my disciples, if you have love for one another."

Part Four:

LIVING IN
BOTH WORLDS

Living in Both Worlds

There is great role confusion in our society today between the preacher and the politician. There are ministers who either act like politicians or plunge directly into the political arena. And there are politicians, with inflated rhetoric about the possibilities of their political programs, who seem to make claims and promises that were once made only by preachers. We seem to be in a new state of confusion as to how the realm of politics interacts with religious faith, if it does at all.

Many today, both on the Right and on the Left, believe that politics is an inevitably corrupting practice that deserves little regard, if not downright contempt. Similarly, many politicians, while not quite believing religion is the opiate of the people, believe that it is not much more than pablum as far as politics is concerned.

To achieve some perspective on this issue, I have found it helpful to consider how past cultures have regarded their politicians, and then to understand some of the philosophical undercurrents which contributed to the foundation of our own pluralistic society.

With this backdrop, I find it possible to set forth tentative views that have grown out of my own experience of relating a personal faith to a political vocation. I hope it may stimulate thought about the imperatives and possibilities of the Christian's relationship to the political realm.

Living in Both Worlds

TWO OUT OF EVERY THREE Americans believe that congressional misuse of government funds is fairly common. So says a recent Gallup poll.

Members of a PTA group in a large suburban high school were once asked to list in order of preference the occupations they would want their children to enter. Doctor and lawyer were at the top. Elected public official was toward the bottom.

In the minds of most people there is a latent suspicion that politicians are somehow dishonest or at least very flexible ethically. Reports of the misconduct of public officials, which always receive front page attention in the newspapers, serve to support the popular notion that all office holders are less than completely honest if not just plain crooked. Disclosures of influence-peddling, misuse of funds, and falsifying government pay records by trusted public servants cause great damage to the people's trust of government officials.

I have often been asked, "How can you be a Christian and be in politics?" There is inherent in this question the popular idea that politics is dirty and that no honest person would get himself involved. Have you ever heard a doctor or a lawyer asked that question? Yet certainly there are as many cases of professional or ethical misconduct in their occupations as among politicians.

The great concern about the malfeasance of an office holder stems, it seems, from three things. The first is the power he can use or misuse in office; that is, his authority to compel obedience to the law and his access to large sums of public money. The second is the concept that an official of the government holds a special trust from the people. He is their representative. He acts with authority delegated from them. He is to serve their—the public's—interests. And third, there is the fact that an office holder lives, so to speak, in a fishbowl. We have come to refer to a government official as being in "public life." There are probing eyes and listening ears to pick up every aspect of a politician's life. Some regard office holders as public property—to be used without regard to personal considerations.

Difficulties in all of these areas come in the ill-defined conflicts of interest. In the use of power, for example, how can a violation of good judgment be distinguished from one of ethics and morals? In the conflict between public and private interests, where is the line to be drawn between clear violations of the law and other "gray" areas where the distinction is not so easy? In the matter of public life, where does privacy become a cover for clandestine activities rather than simply the wish to be left alone?

Our ideals of civic duty and the responsibility of carrying the public trust probably find their origins in the two roots of Western culture—the traditions of Israel and of Greece and Rome. The theological and ideological heritages of these two traditions become immediately apparent. The judges and kings of ancient Israel ruled by appointment from God. Their authority was broad and virtually absolute. We see the origin of human government as an instrument of the will of God in the Scripture.

It is significant, I believe, that we even have recorded in the accounts of the lives of Israel's rulers the details of their flaws and misconduct, both public and private. These misdeeds were viewed as violations of God's commandments. They were even described as breaches of the personal trust and relationship between God and man. When a ruler in Israel was accused of some misconduct he would be condemned for violating God's holy law rather than for simply acting against the public interest. In the economy of the Old Testament, God's will was the public interest.

The history of Israel teaches us another interesting principle: the people could turn to God for relief from an oppressive and evil ruler. Herein lies the seed of the political philosophy of the right of revolution. The idea that a people can appeal to God for protection and justification in altering or overthrowing their unjust government and rulers finds eloquent expression in the documents of the American Revolution. The roots are in ancient Scripture. But we should also be aware that Israel frequently suffered under oppressive rulers as a direct result of its own evil conduct and disobedience to God's commandments. In other words, corrupt and evil government resulted from the moral degeneration of the people themselves. This is a point to remember when we begin to judge the ethical conduct of public officials in our own country.

From the Greeks and from the Romans we inherited our commitment to the ideals of reason, order, and moderation. The public good, the common interest—especially in the Greek city-states—was the principal motivation for

Mark Hatfield

morality in public office. In Athens it was the custom to conduct a public examination (*dokimasia*) of a candidate's character before he could be selected for public office. His entire life was open to challenge by any citizen. He had to prove freedom from physical defect and from scandal, the pious honoring of his ancestors, and the full payment of his taxes. His record of military duty was also closely examined. If he passed these tests and was selected for office, usually by lot, he would swear an oath to perform the obligations of his office and to avoid accepting bribes and presents.

Instruction in the responsibilities of citizenship and the nobility of public service was an essential part of the education of the young men in Athens. The swearing of the Ephebic Oath committed them to high ethical conduct in public service and admitted them to full citizenship in the city. It was expected that every citizen of Athens would serve at least one year in public office. Civic duty was an accepted part of Greek life. Even though the oath of public office was taken on the altars of the Greek gods, a violation of the oath was considered a breach of the public trust, rather than a sin against God—as was the case of Israel.

Thucydides, the Greek historian, reported that the Greeks were more anxious to be called clever than honest, however. There was hardly a man in Athenian public life who was not charged with crookedness. The legend of Diogenes searching with his lantern, when the sun was high, for an honest man may be closer to fact than one realizes.

In the *Republic* Plato proposed a society in which only the most qualified and wise ruled. These philosopher-kings alone knew what was good for men and states. There was no need for law because these wise rulers were the law. In Plato's view these rulers acted for the total good because they alone knew what was absolutely good and right. Pure

Conflict and Conscience   152

reason, embodied in the philosopher-king, prevailed. Plato believed that the purpose of the state was to produce the highest type of human being. This idea ran quite contrary to the deep convictions of the Greeks about the moral value of freedom under the law and of the participation by the citizens in the task of self-government.

Aristotle emphasized the Greek idea of a government of laws rather than of men—no matter how wise and good the men might be. He felt that there should be a moral equality between the ruler and the ruled in that they both must obey the law.

The Greek ideals of public service and civic pride and duty have influenced us to a large extent. Yet the Greeks became loosened from their own ethical traditions. Public morality declined, carried out on the tide of private degeneration.

The Romans built the world's greatest empire on the grand excellence of military might and administrative proficiency. The legions of the emperors were not known for their mercy but for their brutal efficiency. Justice in the courts was accorded only to those fortunate enough to be citizens of the empire. The Christian missionary Paul of Tarsus was one of these. Officials of the Roman Empire were not responsible to the public interest in their conduct of business. Their major allegiance was to the emperor and his provincial governors. With great administrative genius the Romans ruled a diverse and far-flung empire. An elaborate system of inspection and record-keeping was developed to check on the efficiency and honesty of their officials.

In the early years of the empire the Roman philosopher and statesman Cicero articulated the idea of an eternal, unchangeable law which was universally binding upon all peoples. This law, based in right reason, was authored by God. It was natural law. Only irrational men would attempt

Mark Hatfield

to violate it. Cicero insisted that, in the light of this eternal law, all men were equal. The true political state was a community for ethical purposes, and unless it were held together by moral ties, it would be nothing but anarchy on a large scale. The commonwealth—"the affair of the people"—was composed of men united by common agreement about law and rights and participation in mutual advantages. For Cicero, a life of political service was the crown of human happiness and achievement. Reasonable men who were altruistically motivated should be called to public service. He insisted that such individuals would rule with integrity and high ethics.

Seneca, the Roman philosopher and dramatist who lived in the first century of the Christian era, was more pessimistic. He reasoned that because the mass of men were so vicious and corrupt, a despotism was preferable to any form of popular government. He believed, therefore, that a political career had little to offer the good man except the annihilation of his goodness. The good man could do little for his fellows by holding political office. Seneca's idea is quite popular among Americans, both in and out of the churches.

By no means, however, did Seneca feel that the wise and good man ought to withdraw from the community. He insisted, as did Cicero, upon the moral obligation of the good man to offer his services in some capacity or other. He rejected the popular Epicurean idea of pursuing private satisfaction at the cost of neglecting the public interests. Public service in his view did not necessarily have to take the form of political office. A good man could render service to humanity even though he had no political power. Here are the seeds of the unique American idea of voluntary private action for the benefit of the community.

In these experiences and thoughts of the Hebrews and of the Greeks and Romans are the roots of our own ideals

Conflict and Conscience

of political morality and the ethics of public office. These roots reached into medieval Christian Europe. They blossomed, grew, and were pruned by the Renaissance, the Reformation, and the Age of Reason. The seeds of the Old World found new life in the New World, and a society with unique political concepts flourished.

The American concept of politics and of public ethics draws heavily from those ancient ideas of Israel, Greece, and Rome. Ours is a refined combination. It was with great optimism in the perfectibility of man that our founding fathers created the American nation. They recognized that the task of building a new society based on the principles of self-government would require the exercise of the highest and most noble qualities of man. Both the citizen and the public official had to act in a selfless, loyal, and dedicated manner in order to make the new democracy work. This fact was most clearly stated in the closing words of the Declaration of Independence: "And for the support of this Declaration, with a firm reliance on the protection of divine Providence, we mutually pledge to each other our Lives, our Fortunes and our sacred Honor." There is in this simple and eloquent statement the combination of the two concepts of public duty of which we have spoken earlier: reliance on God's protection (Judeo-Christian) and a mutual pledge of life, fortune, and honor for the common or public interest (Greco-Roman).

There was the basic assumption by our nation's authors that a democratic society would free the best spirit within man. This spirit, motivated by God, and educated in biblical truths, could create the greatest good for the greatest number of people. They also recognized that man can be selfish, dishonest, and tyrannical. And so the government was structured to safeguard against tyranny and to protect people from the selfishness of their governors.

Mark Hatfield

Daniel Webster summed up the attitude of the nation's early leaders by saying that "whatever makes men good Christians, makes them good citizens."[1] There was a feeling, a hope that the nobleness and integrity in the spirit of men would rise to the surface in American society. There was even the hope that the spiritual motivation of men could be transferred into a sort of civic religion and zeal for freedom. Whatever it was that made men good Christians and good citizens was to be encouraged and nurtured in the American family, the churches, and the schools in the hope that these qualities of individual life would create the new citizens for the new society.

Our founding fathers, however, were practical men. They had been through experiences which taught them to distrust the nature of man—at least men in political power. Having witnessed tyranny over the mind, the body, and the spirit, they wanted to construct a system of constitutional government to insure that tyranny could not take root in the new world. Therefore, today we have a political system which allows for the peaceful debate between conflicting interests. James Madison in number ten of the *Federalist Papers* explained the function of what we now know as the political parties as the balancing of various group interests against one another in order to arrive at the common good.

We have today a political system that recognizes, in a general way at least, that God rules in the affairs of men. We recognize that a public official is a servant of the people and a trustee of their delegated sovereign power. We acknowledge the need for loyalty to common goals and ideals of government by both officials and citizens of the nation. And we have grown accustomed to expecting our public officials to be men of honor, integrity, and decency.

These are our ideals, our traditions, our roots. But what of our practices, our works? As we weigh our ideals against

Conflict and Conscience   156

our present performance, we find that the scales are tipped out of balance. Our newspaper headlines give us new reasons to suspect that few public office holders are honest. We are stunned to hear a sub-cabinet official state that the government has the right to lie to the people. We hear constantly of the "credibility gap" in government—the distance between the truth and what is told to the nation. Influence-peddling and fraud by government employees and their friends cause us to wonder what has become of integrity in public service.

The standard reaction to all of this by the American public has been to draw a general rule from specific cases and to condemn everyone in public office as a crook. For many who take seriously their moral convictions and Christian faith there is a grave question as to whether a "good man" or a Christian could enter politics and still keep his faith. Because of this, many good, honest people avoid politics and seek "safer" vocations. This approach creates a serious vacuum of morality in places of public leadership.

While condemning their public officials for misconduct, most Americans fail to realize that they are pointing their fingers at the "representatives" of the people. These men hold office because we, the people, put them there. We helped to elect them—the good ones and the bad ones— either by voting or failing to vote; by making our views known or by withholding our comments and complaining only where we could not be heard.

We should remember that the Congress, the executive branch—indeed, government at all levels—are no better than the demands of the citizens. If the people pursue excellence, they can require it from their public officials. If the nation seeks after righteousness, then its leaders should surely point the way. If each of us, as citizens, expects moral and ethical leadership in government, we ought to be prepared to render that kind of service our-

Mark Hatfield

selves whenever called on to do so. By the quality of our own personal ethical and spiritual character we ought to be setting the standards for conduct, both private and public.

There is an old saying, "All that is necessary for evil to triumph is for good men to do nothing." This is precisely where we find ourselves today in the matter of Christian ethics and political morality. For many political generations too many good men have done nothing. They have stood by as neutral observers while the contest was fought in the political arena. This is true in the local community, it is widespread on the state level, and it is certainly the case in national politics.

If the message of the transforming power of God in Christ is applicable to the individual human being, then it must have an effect upon social man and his community. A man's view of the world and his relationships to those around him must change when he is confronted with the message of the gospel. Changed men must build a changed world. Christians must become involved in the processes of transformation in our world as God leads them. One of the major processes for orderly change in our world is politics—the art and science of human government.

For the Christian man to reason that God does not want him in politics because there are too many evil men in government is as insensitive as for a Christian doctor to turn his back on an epidemic because there are too many germs there. For the Christian to say that he will not enter politics because he might lose his faith is the same as for the physician to say that he will not heal men because he might catch their diseases.

John Stuart Mill in chapter two of his treatise on representative government wrote:

If we ask ourselves on what causes and conditions good government in all its senses, from the humblest to the most exalted, depends, we find that the principal of them, the one which transcends all others, *is the qualities of the human beings composing the society over which the government is exercised.*[2] [italics mine]

The American people have made the kind of government which they have today. If there is evil, immorality, and unethical behavior in government, the American people must share in the shame for these conditions. Where there is nobleness, honesty, integrity, and goodness, the American people may take credit for that too.

The solution to the problem of immorality in public office begins with the character of the people of this nation. It must begin with us as we search our hearts and consciences. Ask yourself these questions: "If everyone else in America were just like me, what kind of country would this be? If everyone took the same interest in government that I do, what kind of government would we have? If everyone obeyed the law, including traffic laws, with the same faithfulness that I do, what kind of crime rate would we have? If everyone accepted public service or community work with the same attitude that I do, how much would get done for the public good? If everyone obeyed his conscience and the spiritual commandments of God with the same faithfulness and courage that I do, what kind of world would this be?" John Stuart Mill goes on in his work to say that "whenever the general disposition of the people is such that each individual regards those only of his interests which are selfish, and does not dwell on, or concern himself for, his share of the general interest, in such a state of things good government is impossible."[3]

All will agree that the selfishness of men accounts for most of our social, political, and economic problems. The founders of our nation knew this fact too, and they attempted to construct a political system in which the selfish interests of one group would be balanced off against those

Mark Hatfield

of another. They saw to it that the selfishness, if we may call it that, of the executive branch of government would be balanced with that of the legislative and judicial branches and vice versa. We call this the separation of powers in our government.

Our government "of laws, rather than men" is really an institution in which we have sought to embody in statutes the best of the ideal conduct of men. John Stuart Mill, again in his treatise on representative government, puts it this way:

> All government which aims at being good is an organisa-
> tion of some part of the good qualities existing in the in-
> dividual members of the community for the conduct of its
> collective affairs. A representative constitution is a means
> of bringing the general standing of intelligence and honesty
> existing in the community, and the individual intellect and
> virtue of its wisest members, more directly to bear upon
> the government. . . . Such influence as they do have is the
> source of all good that there is in the government, and the
> hindrance of every evil that there is not. The greater the
> amount of these good qualities which the institutions of a
> country succeed in organising, and the better the mode of
> organisation, the better will be the government.[4]

Though we Americans have sought to organize the best that is in the nation, we find that we have not always suc-ceeded. We see indications that the worst qualities of man appear to gain in power and influence. It is easy to become cynical and mourn the defeat of our idealism. It is this cynicism which causes many Christians to avoid entering public service.

There is a reluctance among those who call themselves Christians to believe that the ultimate victory belongs to Christ. We fail to understand that God is at work in history and that all human affairs will one day be consummated in

Jesus Christ. We have in the revealed truth of God the assurance of his power and the promise of its application in our daily lives. This fact gives us the kind of security and stability which allows us to risk ourselves in the service of mankind. Christ said that it is only when we lose our lives for his sake that we truly find them (Matt. 10:39). It is when we turn our eyes from the anxious anticipation of circumstances surrounding us and lift them to see the power and dominion of God in Christ that we gain the perspective and leverage to change the world in which we live.

The citizen-Christian, then, faces a twofold challenge. First, by obedience to the Great Commission, the teaching of the gospel of Christ, he must redeem the citizens of our society and thereby build a better foundation for government. His second challenge is to be willing to serve God in politics and government if that is where God wants him. The great experiment that is America calls to each generation for the kind of men and women who will dare to make this nation what it was meant to be. The call is to service, to loyalty, to sacrifice, and to opportunity. The crisis is in the dearth of leadership. The greatest need of our times is for men who will give of themselves and who will serve unselfishly in a position of public trust. The call is for leaders who will be led by God.

Let us turn now from this discussion of the citizen's responsibility for morality in government to some thoughts about the relationship of a leader's personal spiritual life to his public service. Of course, the need for personal faith is not limited merely to those involved in public service. The trials, the temptations, the sense of void and loneliness can be present in any person's life, regardless of his profession.

There are certain problems, however, which are perhaps

Mark Hatfield

intensified by a political career. Among these is the temptation of the ego. There are tremendous pressures in public service to fixate upon one's own importance. The man who falls in love with his own image loses all touch with real human needs. He loses all perspective for his own capacities. The political leader with an inflated ego makes no room for God in his life and suffers from the blasphemous delusion that he has no such need. In my own life, I know of no solution except a personal, daily relationship with Jesus Christ. If we cease to believe in a personal deity because of the inflation of our own ego, God does not die, but we die when our lives cease daily to be renewed by the steady radiance of his love. Dag Hammarskjöld wrote: "Your position never gives you the right to command. It only imposes on you the duty of so living your life that others can receive your orders without being humiliated." [5] Men need God in their lives to live in that manner, for the ego is always humbled before God.

Another intensified problem for the public servant is that it is easy to forget what it means to serve. True service permits neither condescension nor exploitation. The imagery of the "public servant" is a fundamental part of the Judeo-Christian tradition. From the servant image of Isaiah to the commands of Christ, we are called to serve others— "the public." Our call to service is not because service has been earned, but rather because each man is of divine worth. Christ provides the example for the Christian in public service. "If I then, your Lord and Teacher, have washed your feet, you also ought to wash one another's feet" (John 13:14, RSV). One's spiritual life should help to renew daily a personal sense of "servanthood."

The personal spiritual life of a public servant should be a constant source of strength. The need for strength is great. Abraham Lincoln admitted: "I have been driven many times upon my knees by the overwhelming conviction that I had nowhere else to go." [6] A daily relationship with God in prayer helps us not to confuse our will with his will. Any person in public life who thinks that he can "go it alone" is tragically mistaken. No man has enough love, enough concern, enough humility, enough strength, enough courage. In an individual's friendship with God there comes each day the humility of having fallen short, the joy of being forgiven, and the strength of being renewed.

Because Christianity is a relationship, not a dogma, it provides a dynamic absolute for one's life. The temptation to lose sight of any absolute is particularly intensified in the political arena. Our democratic system holds that the best political policy is not derived from some political absolute, but formulated through the legal clash of many relative views. In such a system, many political leaders can see no absolute which does not change with the situational context.

I can accept neither simplistic dogmatism nor total relativity. My relationship with Christ gives me a base—an absolute—both for my personal and my public life. This is the one constant factor running through all of life. The dynamics of this relationship can give the Christian both an absolute foundation and the freedom to deal with the relativity of the political sphere. There is a perspective, an equilibrium, and a total world view which the Christian can achieve, and this gives him the capacity to deal with relative and changing circumstances.

Let us turn for a moment to how Christian belief affects the mechanics of government. According to our pledge of allegiance, we are "one nation under God." I think that too often we misunderstand what it means to be "under God." It does not mean that somehow "God is on our side." As Voltaire sarcastically put it: "It is said that God is always for the big battalions." [7] Being "under God" does not mean that our Constitution should affirm a particular faith. Nor does it mean that this country is uniquely under his protection. We have not always been right, and we cannot claim the approval of God upon everything we have done. Thomas Jefferson once said: "I tremble for my country when I reflect that God is just." [8] It is neither necessarily unpatriotic to believe that God could bring his judgment upon the United States of America, nor is it in our best interests to remain silent when we consider government policies and actions wrong. The ancient prophets of Israel certainly did not spare the rod in pointing to the sins of the rulers as well as to those of the people. Like each of us as individuals, our country is of man as well as of God.

A clearer understanding of "under God" is found in the phrase which appears on all our coins: "In *God* we trust." A nation cannot "trust in God" unless its people and its leaders are committed to that trust. Christian belief affects the mechanics of government only as individuals approach the system with this trust. In this connection, two things are important for us to remember. First, there can be no peace where God is not in the hearts of men. This is individual trust. Second, as one man has said, "There will be no peace so long as God remains unseated at the conference table." [9] This is national trust manifested through individuals as they relate to the governmental system. This relationship between individual morality and trust and national ethics and trust is clearly stated in 2 Chronicles 7:14 (RSV): "If my people who are called by my name humble themselves, and pray and seek my face, and turn from their wicked ways," (individual trust and repentance) "then I will hear from heaven, and will forgive their sin and heal their land" (national trust and repentance).

Only when it is "in *God* we trust" will we be able truly to say that we are "one nation *under* God." What does this mean in practical terms? As a public official, I have as much responsibility to the Christian as to the non-Christian. I firmly support the full separation of church and state. Yet, Christ asks each of us to involve ourselves with mankind. This includes a very real responsibility to the institutions of our secular life. The responsibility of the public servant is not to Christianize the institutions of government but to bring the influence of Christ to bear upon them. Whenever we are successful in institutionalizing a particular article of our faith by enacting it into law, we seem to lose the vitality, spirit, and freshness of it. There often is an abdication of our individual responsibility. Christ recognized this human tendency toward institutionalism when he did not encourage Peter to build the three monuments on the Mount of Transfiguration. We cannot capture great spiritual truths in concrete, or in law. Both statues and statutes can become forms of idolatry. No amount of government legislation can replace the function of the church which is to change men's hearts by the power of Christ.

If the Christian faith is to have any effect on the mechanics of government, it must be through the lives of public officials coming together in God. There are numerous opportunities for this throughout our government. The prayer breakfast groups in the Senate and House of Representatives create a kind of fellowship in which we can humble ourselves together before God. There are similar groups of public officials and civic leaders in every state of the Union and in most of the countries of the world. They meet out of a recognition that they need God's guidance and grace in carrying out their public duties. I have had reports of situations in which public policy controversies have been settled when the leaders of the opposing sides were able to reconcile their differences in prayer. A unique spiritual bond is formed between public officials who can come together in prayer before God. I have seen this take place

Mark Hatfield

between leaders of different nations. The personal lives of public men are changed by these encounters with God. This is fundamental; the Christian faith cannot affect the mechanics of government except as it affects the lives of individual men who bear influence on these institutions.

Our view of man and his relationship to the state and the government has been greatly influenced by our Judeo-Christian tradition. We begin with God—as Creator, as Lawgiver. We view man as a divine creation. Not only is each man created by God, but he is also created in the image of God with a creative potential of his own. Christianity affirms that each man is of divine worth. An individual is of infinite worth, not because he earned it but because he is created, sustained, and loved by God. We love each other only because God first loved us. We recognize the value of men as creatures of God having the same direct access to God that we have. Since we believe in our own value as creatures of God, we respect the worth of others.

The state—the institution of human government—has been ordained by God to serve the individual. We must remember that the individual was not ordained to serve the state. It is the duty of government to provide and to permit the opportunities and freedoms by which man can fulfill his creative potential. In this delicate relationship between God, man, and the government, it is easy to lose sight of God. When this happens the relationship between man and government becomes distorted. Governments that lose the view of man as a creature of divine worth often force him to bow to service to the state without regard for his obligation to God. When governments fail to recognize man's allegiance to God, they court revolution. When men fail to recognize their allegiance to God, they court tyranny.

We cannot discuss the subject of Christian ethics and politics without touching briefly upon the question of whether men can be faithful Christians and still differ politically. As to the possibility of this, I have no doubt. There are many fine Christians who disagree with each other on political questions.

This concept often becomes a problem of great concern to some Christians. They cannot understand how a public official could disagree with them on a political issue and still claim to be a Christian. This view is caused, I think, when we allow ourselves to fall into the idolatry of marrying our particular brand of theology to a certain political philosophy. The typical examples of this are the liberal theology-liberal politics blend, and the orthodox theology-conservative politics mixture.

It is dangerous for us to read into the Scripture any particular political point of view. Christ's teachings, and the letters of Paul, are very clear. We must be willing to be disturbed enough by what we read in the Bible to allow the Spirit of God to change us as individuals so that we may change our world.

We must also recognize the ultimate hand of God in the affairs of men. If two Christians disagree on a matter of political policy, they both could be wrong. They both need to recognize that God is at work in history and that his will is to be accomplished regardless of their political opinions. Our duty must remain that of being faithful to God above all else and following him as he guides us through prayer, the Scripture, and the Holy Spirit. Ultimately, we shall see as we are seen and then God will show us the breadth of his will and the extent of his kingdom. And the great question asked of us will not be whether we stood on the right or on the left, politically, but whether we stood in the shadow of the Cross of Christ.

No matter how we regard the politics of our government, the commandment of Christ and the teaching of Paul indicate clearly that we are to obey the appointed authorities in all points over which they have rightful authority. Christ

Mark Hatfield

admonished his questioners to "render to Caesar the things that are Caesar's, and to God the things that are God's" (Luke 20:25, RSV). Paul exhorted Timothy:

> First of all, then, I urge that supplications, prayers, intercessions, and thanksgivings be made for all men, for kings and all who are in high positions, that we may lead a quiet and peaceable life, godly and respectable in every way. This is good, and it is acceptable in the sight of God our Savior (1 Tim. 2:1–3, RSV).

It is much easier for us to criticize and condemn our public officials than it is for us to pray for them. We find it difficult to pray for those with whom we disagree. Yet this is God's will in order that "we may lead a quiet and peaceable life, godly and respectable in every way."

This is a practical point of departure from which we can begin to have an influence upon our government and upon its public officials. Prayer changes men. Your prayers can change men who make history. Your faithfulness to God as a citizen and as a Christian can mean the difference in the destiny of the United States of America—"one nation under God."

The telephone rang one evening when all
our family was gathered around the dining
room table. My son, MarkO, answered it and
said, "Dad, it's the White House." With cautious
curiosity I picked up the phone. In a few
moments President Richard M. Nixon came onto
the line.

"Mark, at our church service this Sunday at
the White House we want to express our prayers
for the astronauts who are on their way to the
moon . . . and we want the whole service to
be directly around the hopes and desires we all
have for peace . . . so I was wondering if you
could come and offer the prayer."

I was a little surprised and deeply honored.
The prayer that follows was given that Sunday
morning, July 20, 1969, when Astronauts Neil
Armstrong and Edwin E. (Buzz) Aldrin, Jr.
landed on the moon while Michael Collins
maneuvered the space capsule.

Our Father, we marvel as three brave space pioneers
prepare for landing on the moon. From the depths of our
hearts we pray for the safe return of Neil Armstrong, Edwin Aldrin, and Michael Collins. Sustain their wives, their
children, and their families during these anxious days. We
are grateful for the thousands of support personnel who
literally are "their brothers' keepers." Excite our imagination to transfer this genius of cooperation and spirit of
teamwork to our many other needs, lest our success on
the moon mock our failures on the earth.

Even as our astronauts go to the moon in the name of

peace, our world aches from the pain of wars. We perfect the means for destroying human life and then believe we have found security. May the nations trust not in the power of their arms but in the Prince of Peace, your Son.

O God, grant us deliverance from the rhetoric of peace when we personally are not willing to do the things which make for peace . . . to love, to forgive, to use wisely all of your gifts and resources for the good of mankind, and to permit the invasion of the Holy Spirit in the lives of each of us so that peace may be reflected in our homes between husbands and wives, between children and parents, and in commerce between management and labor, between citizens and government, and among all races of men.

O Lord, keep us mindful that technical success does not necessarily produce wisdom. We pray for wisdom for our president and for all who govern this nation—the true wisdom that is found described by James as, "The wisdom that comes from God is first utterly pure, then peace-loving, gentle, approachable, full of tolerant thoughts and kindly actions, with no breadth of favoritism or hint of hypocrisy. And the wise are peacemakers who go on quietly sowing for a harvest of righteousness—in other people and in themselves" (James 8:17–18, Phillips).

We pray for this in the name of your Holy Son, our Savior Jesus Christ.

AMEN.

NOTES

DEAR SENATOR

1. Jacques Ellul, *The Presence of the Kingdom*, trans. Olive Wyon (Philadelphia: Westminster, 1951), p. 13.

THE (HOLY?) SPIRIT OF '76

1. Alexis De Tocqueville, *Democracy in America*, ed. Richard D. Heffner (New York: Mentor, 1956), pp. 144–45.
2. James Madison, *Federalist Papers*, No. 51.
3. Thomas Hutchinson, *History of the Colony of Massachusetts Bay* (London: n.p., 1760), 1:501.
4. John Higginson, quoted in T. J. Wertenbaker, *The Puritan Oligarchy* (New York: Charles Scribner's Sons, 1946), p. 202.
5. Francis Bowen, in *The American Political Economy* (New York: Charles Scribner's, 1870), p. 21.
6. *The Nation*, 1886, 42:419.
7. Pierre Berton, *The Comfortable Pew* (New York: J. B. Lippincott Co., 1965), p. 80.
8. Robert S. Lynd and Helen Merrill Lynd, *Middletown in Transition, A Study of Cultural Conflicts* (New York: Harcourt, Brace & Co., 1937), p. 316.
9. *Gallup Poll Report 35* (Princeton, N.J.: Gallup Institute, Inc., May 1968), p. 23.
10. Michael Novak, *A Theology for Radical Politics* (New York: Herder & Herder, 1969), pp. 17–18.

TO HEAL THE WORLD

1. John D. Montgomery, *Foreign Aid in International Politics* (Englewood Cliffs, N.J.: Prentice-Hall, 1967), p. 63.

FROM CURIOSITY TO COMMITMENT

1. David Poling, *Last Years of the Church* (New York: Doubleday & Co., 1969).

LIVING IN BOTH WORLDS

1. Daniel Webster, *The Writings and Speeches of Daniel Webster* (Boston: Little, Brown, 1903), 1:220.

2. John Stuart Mill, *Considerations on Representative Government* (Oxford: Basil Blackwell, 1940), p. 125.

3. Ibid., p. 126.

4. Ibid., pp. 128–29.

5. Dag Hammarskjöld, *Markings* (New York: Alfred A. Knopf, 1964)), p. 105.

6. Abraham Lincoln, quoted in Noah Brooks, "Personal Recollections of Abraham Lincoln," *Harper's*, July 1865, p. 226.

7. *Oeuvres Complètes de Voltaire* (Paris: Garnier Frères, 1882), 46:551.

8. Thomas Jefferson, *Notes on the State of Virginia* (Philadelphia: Pritchard and Hall, 1788), p. 173.